the BIG BAG BOOK

By Carter Houck and Myron Miller

The Big Bag Book
American Quilts and How to Make Them

the BIG BAG BOOK

Carter Houck and Myron Miller

Charles Scribner's Sons   New York

Many thanks to the staffs of museums and companies who made this book easier and more fun.
The Museum of Contemporary Crafts, The Museum of the American Indian, The Metropolitan Museum of Art, The American Museum of Natural History, David Traum Notions, William Wright Trimmings, Loewenthal Trimmings, Pacific Mills Division of M. Lowenstein & Sons, The Pellon Corporation, and Skinner Fabrics, Springs Mills, Inc.

The author, Carter Houck, and photographer, Myron Miller, dedicate this book to each other for having the patience to produce a second volume together.

LINE ART BY FRANCINE DEL RE

Copyright © 1977 Carter Houck and Myron Miller

Library of Congress Cataloging in Publication Data

Houck, Carter.
    The big bag book.

    1. Handbags. 2. Tote bags. I. Miller, Myron, 1918- II. Title.
TT667.H68   646.4'8   77-7163
ISBN 0-684-15180-4
ISBN 0-684-15179-0 pbk.

This book published simultaneously in the
United States of America and in Canada—
Copyright under the Berne Convention

All rights reserved. No part of this book
may be reproduced in any form without the
permission of Charles Scribner's Sons.

1 3 5 7 9 11 13 15 17 19 MD/C 20 18 16 14 12 10 8 6 4 2
1 3 5 7 9 11 13 15 17 19 MD/P 20 18 16 14 12 10 8 6 4 2

Printed in the United States of America

Contents

Introduction		1
1	Tricks of the Trade	9
2	Basic Shapes and Things to Come	24
3	The Great Easy Tote Bag	37
4	The Square Root of All Bags	48
5	Handles Without Care	53
6	Sport Your Own Bag	57
7	Packing It In	69
8	Fold, Roll, and Picnic in the Park	76
9	Have Bag—Will Travel	82
10	Treasured Playthings	91
11	Store It Softly	97
12	Practical Purses	100
13	Glitter a Little	108
14	From Grandma's Scrap Bag	113
15	Yours Personally	122
16	Cheap, Quick Fun	133
17	Everything Is Fair Game	142
Sources		151

the BIG BAG BOOK

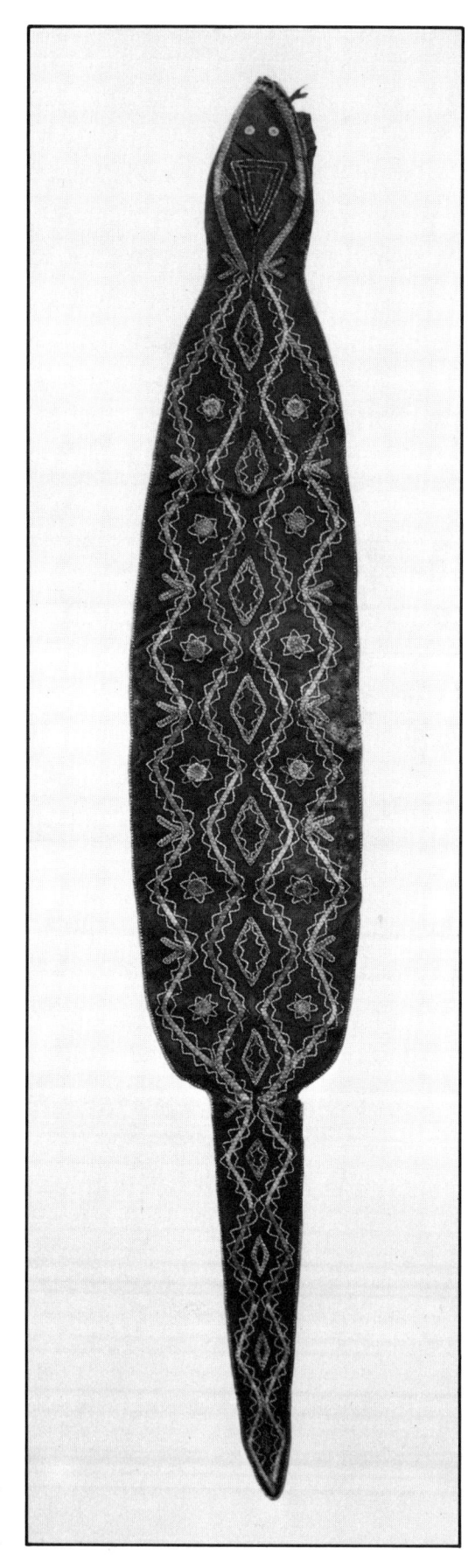

Medicine bag, made of buckskin in the shape of an otter and decorated with quills. Courtesy of the Museum of the American Indian.

Introduction

BAGS FROM LONG AGO

In recent years archeologists and researchers have spent a lot of time and millions of words telling us about man's superiority. Equipped with a large brain and an opposing thumb, early man was soon on his way to civilization. The fact that he could carry things in his hands at all must have led him at an early stage to realize that he could never carry as much as he wanted. When he found a bush overflowing with berries, his two hands were inadequate to the task of carrying home all that he could pick.

There is strong evidence that his brain worked to solve such problems long before he would record his history. Perhaps he found a large leaf, laid the berries in the center, and pulled the edges carefully together. He could carry three or four leaves full of fruit and be way ahead of his neighbor who came home with only two handfuls of berries for his hungry children. Certainly animal skins took their place as carriers almost as soon as they were worn for warmth. After that, long strands of grass were woven together into soft mats which could be pulled up at the corners and perhaps tied and hung on the ends of sticks.

The invention of the needle changed fashion radically and bags went right along with clothes. When the corners of a mat could be pulled together and a seam made down each side, more could be carried with less danger of some of it falling out. Though the original square pulled together at the corners never quite died away, bags progressed in size, shape, and usefulness side by side with wearing apparel.

Decoration became a large part of bag making. Sometimes the designers seem to have lost sight of the purpose and practicality, going on wild sprees of painting, embroidering, beading, and bejeweling every kind of bag.

In many highly civilized countries bags became status symbols, just as they did in tribal life. The medicine man had a special bag with magic properties which awed lesser members of the tribe. But was that very different from the effect created by the doctor's bag, back when doctors made house calls and awed their patients?

2   THE BIG BAG BOOK

The medicine man's bag was often covered with such valuables as feathers from rare birds, intricately beaded symbols, and heads of small animals. It was sometimes made in the shape of an animal or was the whole skin of an animal carefully cured to retain its shape. Such works of art fortunately still remain to be seen in many museums, especially those devoted to the American Indian.

In every part of the world some version of the small belt purse can be found. These were, and still are, worn by men and women alike. The Roman man's toga was folded and draped in such a way as to create a large "sinus" or pocket for carrying the daily necessities. But in later centuries, European costume was close fitted, allowing no room for pockets, so that the hip belt came into being with a purse on a chain dangling from it. In Scottish highland costume the sporran still hangs on a chain on the front of the pocketless kilt. From the time of arrows to the time of powder and shot, men often had bags for ammunition dangling from belt or shoulder. Women in medieval times hung scissors, keys, and other

Otter hide pouch, decorated with false wampum, tin danglers, and red-dyed deer hair ends (1790–1795). Courtesy of the Museum of the American Indian.

Medicine bag or buffalo bundle, decorated with cut and scraped designs and white beads. Courtesy of the Museum of the American Indian.

Peruvian cotton bag with designs both woven and painted. From the collection of the American Museum of Natural History. Photo courtesy of the American Crafts Council.

symbols of housewifery along with tiny purses from their belts. The more things a woman suspended from her waist, the more affluent she was.

In periods when clothes were full enough for pockets to be hidden in them, bags lost their importance but not necessarily their meaning as part of fashion. From medieval times through the Victorian era ladies knitted and netted, crocheted and embroidered, beaded and generally overdecorated tiny purses, more to prove their ability as needlewomen than to make bags which served any useful purpose. During the nineteenth century, when the slim Empire gown was fashionable, the reticule made its appearance and remained on through the century even though skirts became enormous enough to hide a dozen pockets.

Just a glance back through paintings and illustrations of Western civilization shows the importance of bags. The English country gentleman used an elegant shoulder bag for the game he shot, whereas the poacher hid his deep in a cloth sack just like the one he used for dragging

China silk bag, elaborately embroidered and decorated. From the collection of the Costume Institute of the Metropolitan Museum of Art. Photo courtesy of the American Crafts Council.

Silk bag from India with chain stitch embroidery. From the collection of the Costume Institute of the Metropolitan Museum of Art. Photo courtesy of the American Crafts Council.

home coal or grain. The prosperous merchant's wife displayed her social position by the chatelaine bag and keys suspended from her belt, while her servant girl ran along the street carrying her purchases in her apron, pulled up at the corners like the first bag that ever existed. Couriers carried important papers, money, and documents in saddlebags and, as Americans pushed west, they usually carried their weapons in holsters, and their ammunition in bullet pouches to make sure that everything arrived intact. The westward movement later produced another familiar figure, the hobo with his worldly goods tied in a bandanna and hanging on a stick over his shoulder, which brings us full circle to that first bag ever which never quite disappears.

In Asia and Africa and every corner of the world bags changed as civilization progressed. Women who worked in the fields carried their babies in large bags slung over the shoulder or in the middle of the back. The grain that was being sowed was frequently carried in a shoulder pouch that hung down at hip level, easy to reach with each swinging motion that scattered the grain. There were skin bags for water and wine, string bags that expanded enormously to accommodate a month's supply of purchases from some distant marketplace, saddlebags for long journeys, all forerunners of today's fashions in bags.

Today, as yesterday, in sophisticated cities as in tribal villages, bags are practical, beautiful, and indispensable to our way of life. They can be made plain and businesslike or decorated and personalized. They can be made of elegant and expensive fabrics or of throwaway muslin. There is no end to the use of bags or to the artistic statement of the bag maker.

BAGS TODAY AND WHY

Suddenly everyone is carrying, or in some cases, wearing, a bag or several bags. It is not unusual to see a woman with a purse, a shopping bag, and a briefcase. Men have become aware of the slovenly look of bulging pockets and are turning to gentlemen's handbags or shoulder bags as well as the attaché case, which has been around for a long time.

Tote bags and shopping bags have become indispensable to our mobile society. Now that we've become used to ease and practicality in our clothes, we even pack them in tote bags. This casual approach to travel has affected suitcases so that they have also become softer and lighter, easier to stuff to the bursting point and cram into an overpacked car.

Every sports enthusiast has a favorite bag, made to hold a tent or compartmentalized to accommodate each piece of tennis gear. Hikers and skiers use backpacks and belt packs in all sizes and shapes. Beach bags of all kinds make a day in the sun more fun with less effort. They may open out into mats to lie on or game boards for checkers, chess, or backgammon.

Household bags are as useful as ever, perhaps more so as space becomes more limited and we have to think of storing things neatly. Shoe bags and garment bags not only organize closets but also help to protect the contents from city smog and furnace smoke. Children's rooms stay cleaner and tidier when there are individual laundry bags for the dirty socks under the bed and the T-shirts on the chairs. There is no reason why a bag can't be made to fit any piece of china or silver or infrequently used treasure.

Making your own may be the best way to get the exact bag you want for a special purpose. You can measure and fit, use the fabric you like in the color you want, and with a few simple seams, you will have a custom-made bag. Once you get into bag making, you will become increasingly creative and original. You can match purses and totes to your costumes, decorate them with embroidery and patchwork, or personalize them with monograms.

For the "friend who has everything" a bag makes a welcome gift. Boat bags, tote bags, game bags, planned to fit a friend's personality and needs, can be made in the time it usually takes you to shop for a gift. You can even make a gift bag to present a gift in, and as inexpensively as you can buy wrapping paper and ribbon.

The bags in this book are flexible in size; dimensions are given for the ones pictured, with suggestions for changes. Many of them can be made from leftover pieces of fabric from your other sewing, anything from slipcover prints and upholstery brocades to bits of synthetic suede and lamé. You can start with patterns but you'll soon be inventing your own variations.

Today's shopping bags are a sign of affluence and super chic.

1
Tricks of the Trade

If you're to become a professional bag maker, you must, like a shoemaker or a sailmaker, know all the little tricks of the trade. They range from choosing the right materials to planning the perfect size and shape. In between you must know what kinds of zippers and trims are suitable, and how to make a quick pocket or pop a lining in.

This chapter attempts to cover all these tricks in three sections, each of which can be read through quickly. In later chapters references will be made to specific techniques—the third section of this chapter—but we strongly suggest that you read the whole chapter once over before starting.

EQUIPMENT:

Very little special equipment is needed for making bags of the type in this book. Many of them can be made by hand as well as on the **sewing machine** so that even a machine is not a necessity. If you do prefer a machine—and you certainly will if you're going into mass production—it can be almost any heavy-duty machine, including Grandma's treadle. Many of the bags in this book were made on a very sturdy **straight-stitch** portable. There are some zigzag techniques mentioned as optional choices, but even they can be done on the most basic type of **zigzag machine.**

One warning about **sewing machines!** If you plan to make the heavy canvas bags, you will need a heavy needle—size 16 or even 18—in your machine. Your machine will always operate better if it is cleaned and oiled, for if it has not been cared for, it may not be able to stitch on heavy or difficult fabrics. Run test pieces of canvas, suede, vinyl, or any problem fabric through before starting to stitch on the bag itself. Using your machine manual as a guide, adjust switch, tension, pressure, or whatever to suit fabric.

Sharp cutting **shears** are the real necessity of bag making. There is no reason for using pinking shears, but have your straight shears sharpened before trying to cut the more difficult fabrics. We like one pair of extra-large heavy ones for the canvas and other heavy materials and a smaller pair for the regular clothing weights.

You will need strong, sharp dressmaker **pins** to hold seams together

10   THE BIG BAG BOOK

while stitching. In vinyls and synthetic leathers pins make marks, so use small **paper clips** or narrow **double-sided tape.**

Short **needles,** about size 5 to 7, are best for hand sewing. In working by hand on the carpeting and vinyl, you may want an even heavier needle. One thing that many bag makers discover for the first time in their sewing experience is that they must use a **thimble** or risk puncturing their hands. **Beeswax** for rubbing on the thread is another aid to tough hand sewing.

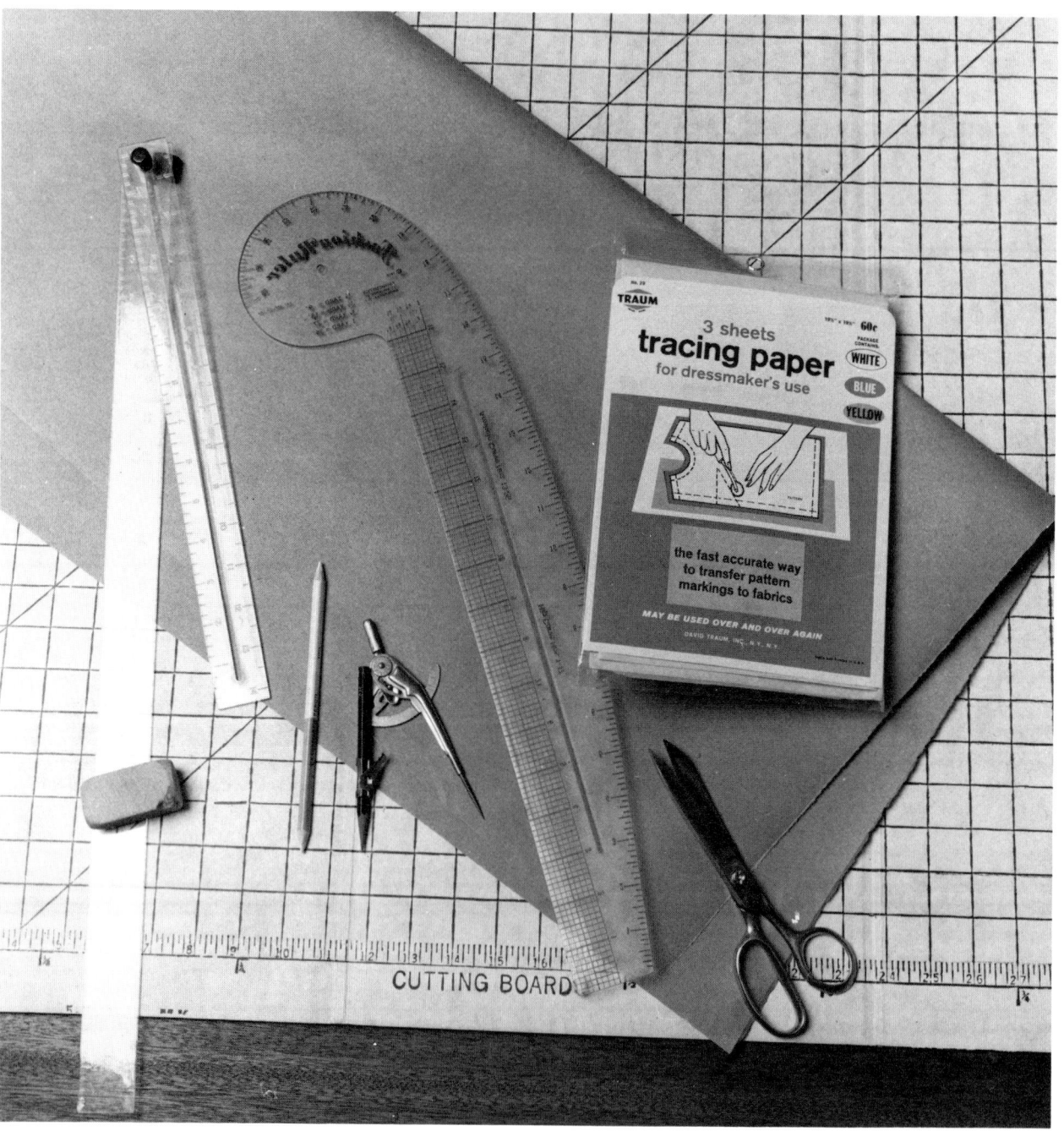

Before you start sewing, you need some simple **drafting tools**. A **ruler** of at least 18 inches or a **yardstick** is indispensable. We like the transparent variety and find the Fashionetics one that turns into an L- or T-square covers several needs in one. A **curve** and a **compass** are useful, though plates and other housewares can be used for drawing circles and curves. Once again we find that the Fashionetics dressmaker's curves are compact and accurate. The sort of compass that children buy for school is perfectly adequate.

A medium soft **pencil** and a white **dressmaker pencil** are good for drawing patterns and designs directly onto fabric. If you need to remove pencil lines, use **art gum eraser.** Another way of transferring designs, especially for embroidery, is with **dressmaker carbon** and a blunt point, like a small knitting needle. Do not use regular carbon on fabric.

If you wish to trace designs or work over the graphs in the back of this book—as you would for enlarging the monograms—use **transparent tracing paper** or **vellum.** Both of these are available in pads of various sizes in stationery and art-supply stores. To make the patterns for the bag shapes themselves, you can use **brown wrapping paper, newspaper,** or anything that's handy.

One other piece of extremely useful equipment is a **cutting board.** This is marked out in squares and inches with grain lines and bias lines indicated to take some of the guesswork out of handling fabric. You can hold your fabric in place on it with heavy pins or **push-pins.** A cutting board protects the table top from pin and scissor scratches. It is a necessity at any time when you wish to cut leathers or vinyls with a razor blade.

PLANNING AND BUYING FABRICS AND TRIMS:

Part of the fun of bag making is that you can use all sorts of odd materials and trimmings, so we can't hope to cover the field in this chapter. We can offer a few suggestions and some useful hints.

Our first piece of advice for making more practical and longer-lasting bags is to be sure that everything used in a bag is compatible. If the **outer fabric** is washable, the **lining, interfacing,** and **trimming** must be also. It is wise to dip all these pieces in warm water ahead of time to make sure that they are completely preshrunk. If you are in doubt about the color-fastness of braid or trim, dip it and lay it on a white towel or paper towel to see that it doesn't bleed.

If the fabric is not washable, there is less to be concerned about. A wool bag which can be dry-cleaned may be lined with almost anything you like, provided that it is dry-cleanable. Buttons, buckles, and handles must also be dry-cleanable or removable. Bags made of vinyl and other materials that are cleaned with a damp sponge may be better with no lining. If you choose to line them, use a dark fabric as we did for the straw beach bag on page 149. Such fabrics—intended for use in home decoration—are often treated for spot and stain resistance, or you can treat them with a spray.

12 THE BIG BAG BOOK

We found that there are so many marvelous **denims** on the market that you might want to make bags of nothing else. They're washable, durable, and come in other colors than blue. On page 144 we even used the unworn parts of several pairs of old jeans.

The **unbleached fabrics** are fun and useful too. Unbleached muslin is inexpensive enough for the gift bags (Chapter 16) and can be decorated in a host of quick and inexpensive ways. Most fabric shops carry heavier unbleached denim and canvas, with all the qualities of endurance, washability, and a nice unbroken surface for decorating that make them the first choice of bag makers. If you want really heavy canvas, you may have to look in sailmaker, farm-supply, or hardware stores. The list of suppliers (page 151) tells where you may order canvas.

Sailcloth, poplin, and **chino** come in bright, washable colors and are heavy enough in texture for many of the large bags. Other sturdy fabrics that have texture rather than color interest are **wool, corduroy, burlap,** and **synthetic leather.** The home-decorating fabric department is a gold mine for bag makers. There are heavy **brocades** for handbags, **cotton-blend tweeds** for totes, soft **linen prints** for gathered knitting bags, and a wealth of **washable cotton-blend prints** and **solids** with appeal and endurance. Try camping outfitters for sturdy fabrics in interesting textures and bright colors.

Drawstring purses and evening bags can be made of leftovers from dresses and evening wear. **Velvets** and **glitter fabrics** are the most popular for evening bags. Solid-color **silks** and **satins** can be decorated with braid and beading just as the Victorian ladies did it. A summer cotton bag for the senior prom can be covered with ruffles.

There are a number of **interfacings** available, but one of the most satisfactory is **nonwoven Pellon®**. It comes in so many weights and some varying textures and can be washed or dry-cleaned endlessly. It has the added advantage of no woven grain so that it can be cut in any direction, making it economical and practically trouble free. There are several weights, from the delicate **Featherweight** to the thick, fluffy **Fleece.** The so-called all-bias Pellon® has slight stretch—better for soft, gathered bags —and the regular is quite stiff—just right for big totes and briefcases. The Fleece gives a nicely padded feeling and is especially attractive in quilted surfaces.

Fusibles are useful in bag making. Pellon interfacings come with a

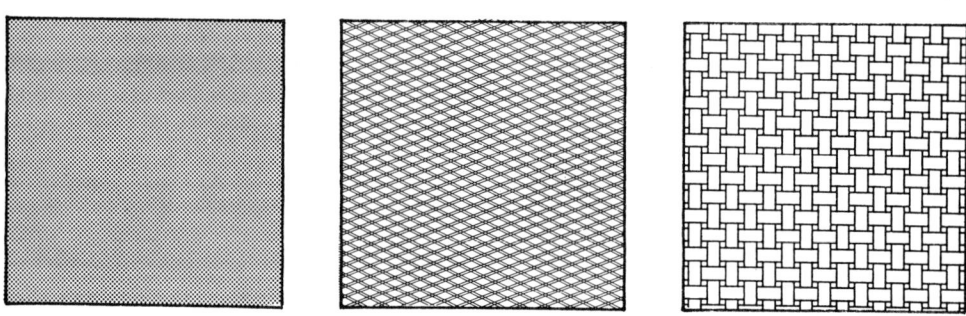

Key: *Wrong side*　　　*Bias*　　　*Fold-braid*

Tricks of the Trade 13

fusible backing so that they can be ironed onto the fabric and will stay there. There is also a **fusible web**—in sheets or strips—which can be used to attach interfacing or to hold hems or pockets in place until they're stitched.

Linings are pretty and practical in that they cover all the raw seams and give a smooth, professional appearance—especially to open bags like totes. Lining should be chosen for its compatibility with the outer fabric. We've already mentioned washability and so on, but the lining should also be in a matching or pleasantly contrasting color. Small calico prints are especially suitable to denims and heavy cottons. It is usual for a lining to be of a lighter weight than the outer fabric.

Trims are for decoration, but on bags they can also serve a useful purpose as handles or straps. Like linings they must be chosen for complete compatibility to the fabric. If they are to be used as handles and are to carry a great deal of weight, look for sturdy woven braids and tapes. If you are doubtful about the carrying capacity of the braid that you want to use, you might back it with strong grosgrain ribbon. If you use a fold-braid or bias binding around the edge and continue it across as a handle, you will also need ribbon or twill tape to reinforce that area.

Cord for drawstrings can be bought at some notions counters but a wider variety will be found in home-decorating fabric departments. The usual size is from $1/4$-inch to $1/2$-inch diameter. Washable cotton bags look quite proper with plain **cotton cable-cord** drawstrings. The **silky cord**—meant for trimming elegant draperies—is handsome on dressy purses like velvet. There are now some attractive novelty cords that imitate macramé.

Zippers are often exposed to view in bags, so it can be fun to use heavy brass or novelty plastic ones and contrasting colors. **Invisible zippers** are perfect if you don't want the zipper to be on display. If you need a zipper shorter than you can find—for a closed pocket, for instance—don't go on a long and fruitless search. Any of the synthetic zippers—regular or invisible—can be cut off at the bottom. Check the package instructions to make sure.

Most bags can be stitched with the same sewing thread that you always use. There is also heavy-duty thread sold in decorator fabric stores, and there is an extra-strong button and carpet thread available for some hand sewing.

Lining

Interfacing

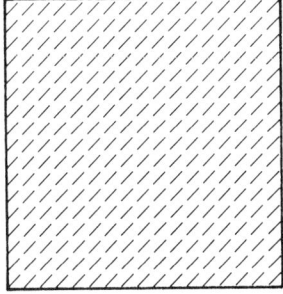

Fusibles

Twill tape

14 THE BIG BAG BOOK

CONSTRUCTION:

We include in this section only the techniques that are specifically used in the construction of these bags. Any general sewing techniques or terms can be found in a basic sewing book.

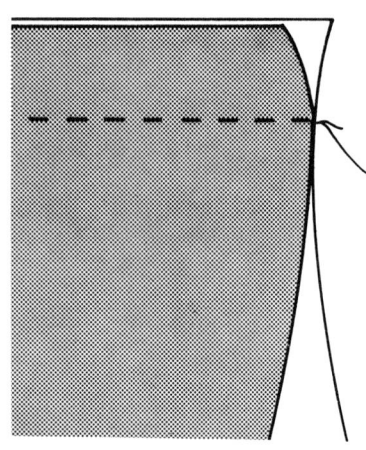

We will start by explaining that when we say to **seam** something, we mean to put the right sides of the fabric together, pin crosswise, and stitch ½ inch from the edge. When we give dimensions for a bag, that is the width of seam allowed. If you plan to use **interfacing,** fuse or machine baste it to the wrong side of the fabric first so that the two layers will be held in the seam together. If the interfacing seems bulky, trim it back to ⅛ inch from the stitching.

The other way in which edges are joined is with a **braid** or **binding** outside. In this case a seam is not always allowed. Lay the pieces wrong sides together—including interfacing, if you plan to use it—and stitch ¼ inch from the edge. Encase the edge in braid or binding as described below.

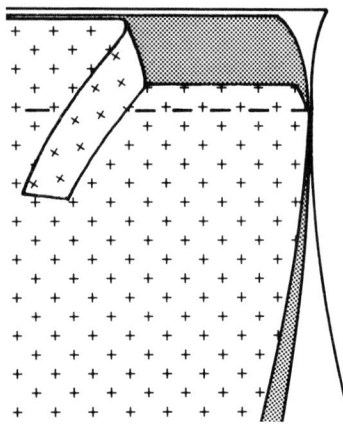

For the purpose of making bags we have simplified the ways of handling **bias binding** and **fold-braid** by giving only two methods. The first one is the one you will use the most. Commercial fold-braid finishes about ½ inch to ⅝ inch wide, which is just perfect for edging bags. If you cut bias strips 2¼ inches wide, the finished effect will be about the same width as the fold-braid.

Lay fold-braid wrong side down to the fabric about ½ inch from the raw edge and edgestitch it in place. Fold it over the edge of the

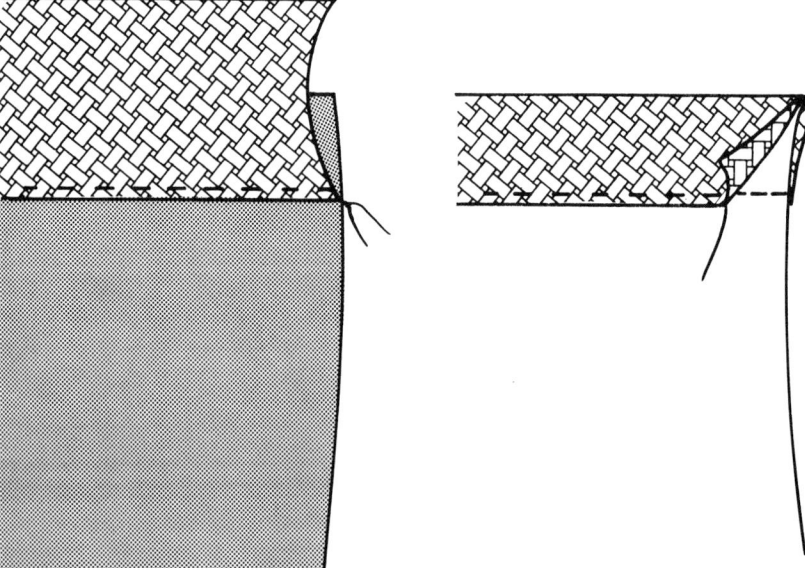

fabric so that it covers the stitching on the other side, press and pin or baste it in place, and edgestitch again.

Lay bias binding right side down to the fabric, raw edges together,

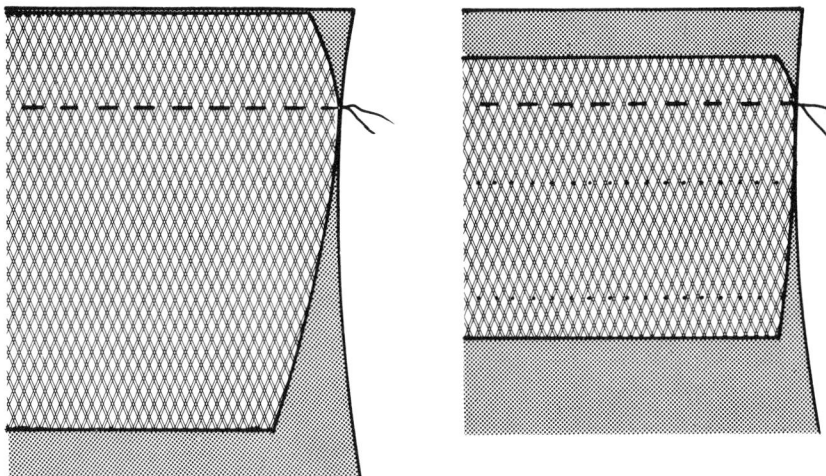

and stitch a 1/2-inch seam. Fold it up and over the edge. Turn the opposite edge under 1/2 inch so that it covers the stitching on the other side, press and pin or baste it in place, and edgestitch it.

In both types of edging the second stitching should come through onto the first side so that the sides look, as nearly as possible, identical. A wide zigzag or zigzag-pattern stitch can be used for added decoration. If the upper edge tends to creep or wrinkle as you stitch, try laying a narrow strip of fusible web under the edge and pressing it in place first.

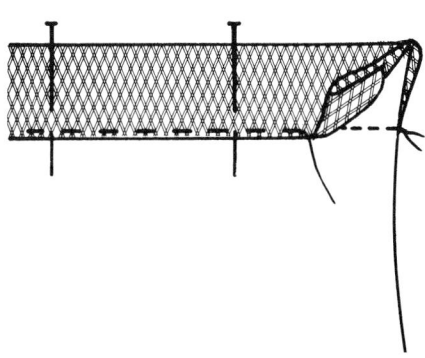

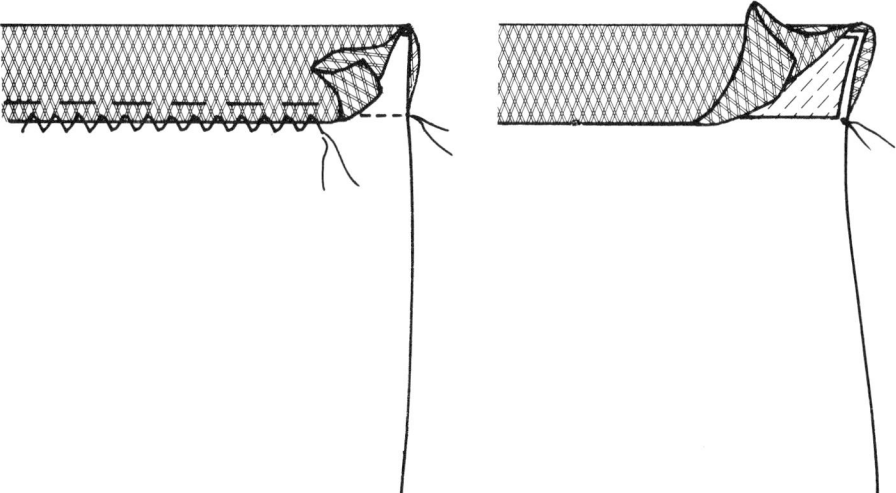

A slight variation can be used for bias binding, so that no machine edgestitching appears on the most important or highly visible side of the bag. We have used this on the boxed bags, finishing it onto the gusset or boxing strip. Start the binding as you did before. Turn under a little less on the second edge and make sure that the folded edge laps nearly

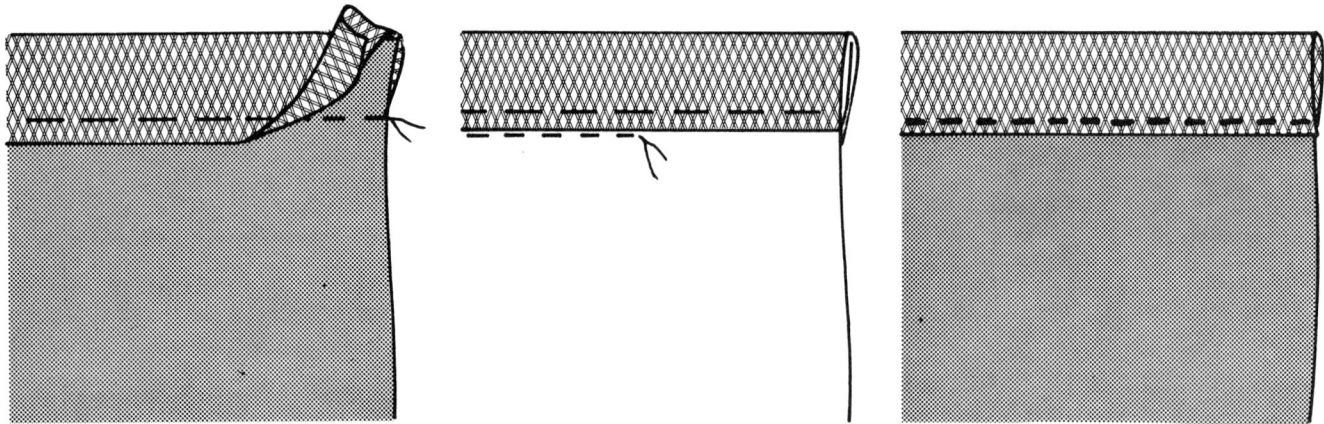

⅛ inch over the first stitching. This will be easier if you baste it in place after pressing. Stitch from the important side, as close as possible to the fold of the binding along the first seam, but not through the binding. On the less important side the stitching should go through the folded edge of the binding, looking very much as it does in the first method.

A variation of this binding used on heavy fabrics leaves the under edge raw. Seam the binding along the edge of the fabric. Fold it over the edge, pin it in place with the raw edge down against the wrong side of the fabric. Machine stitch from the right side, as close to the binding as possible, through the bag and the under layer of the binding. This can be used only as an edge finish, not on an outside seam as just described.

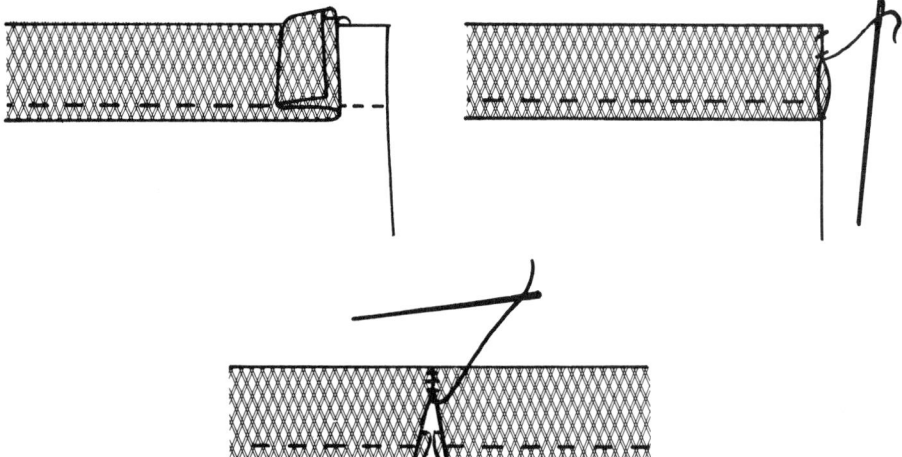

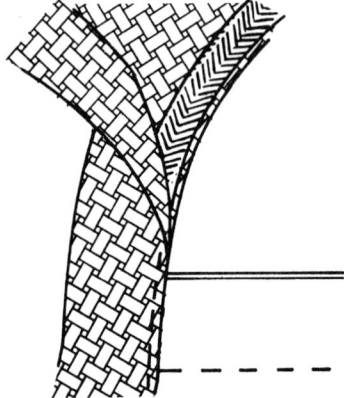

The end of binding can always be finished by turning under ½ inch and slipstitching. If the binding meets at the ends, turn both ends under and slipstitch them together.

If **braid** or **bias binding** continues across as a **handle,** lay narrow **grosgrain ribbon** or **twill tape** inside for reinforcement before stitching the edges together. Fusible web may be useful here too.

There are two kinds of **pockets** that can be used easily on bags—the **simple patch** and the **closed zipper patch.** Use them inside on the lining or outside on the bag. A **simple patch** can be cut to any size desired, plus

½-inch seams on three sides and 1½-inch hem on the fourth. Finish the edge of the hem with a ½-inch fold or with stitching, depending on the weight of the fabric. Turn the hem back, rights sides together, onto the pocket and seam the ends. Trim the corners and turn the hem right side out. Pin and stitch the hem in place. Fold the remaining seam allowance under and press. Pin the pocket in place on the bag and edgestitch. At the top corners, you may wish to stitch a reinforcement as is used on a man's shirt pocket.

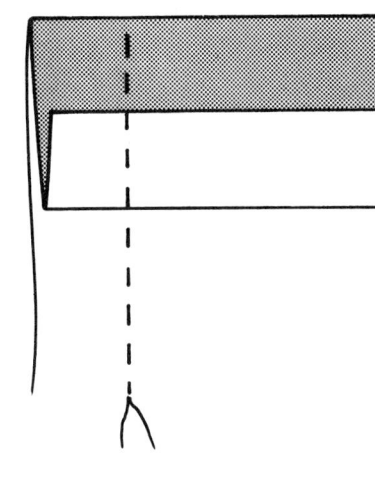

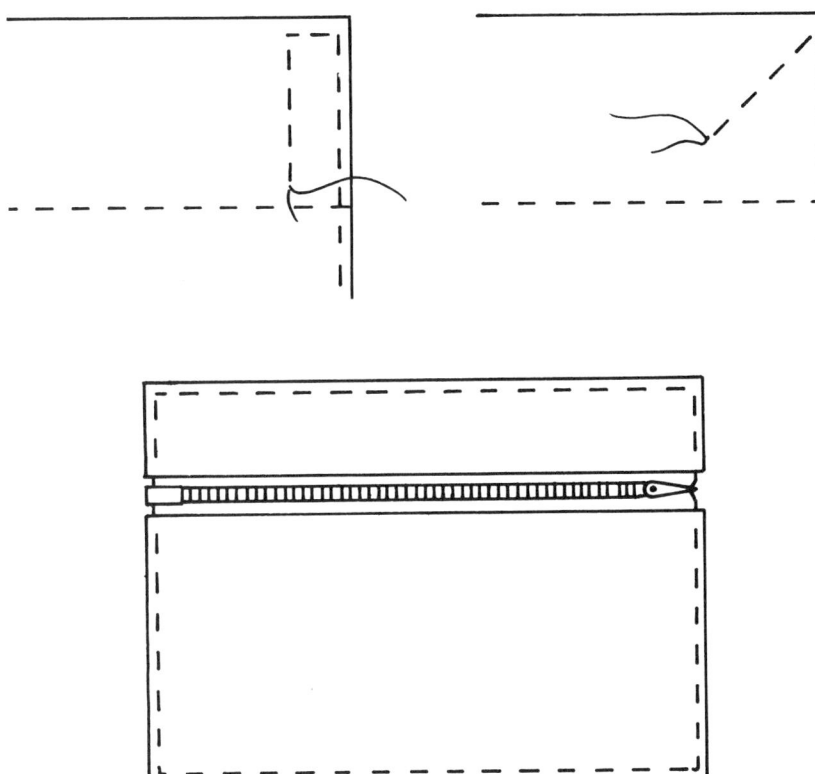

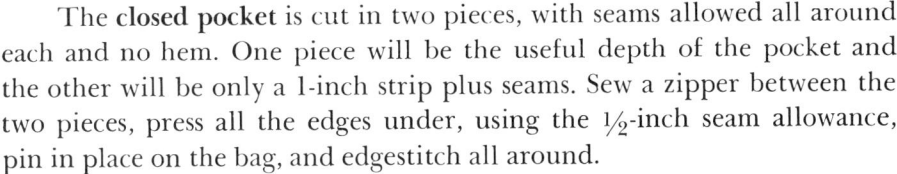

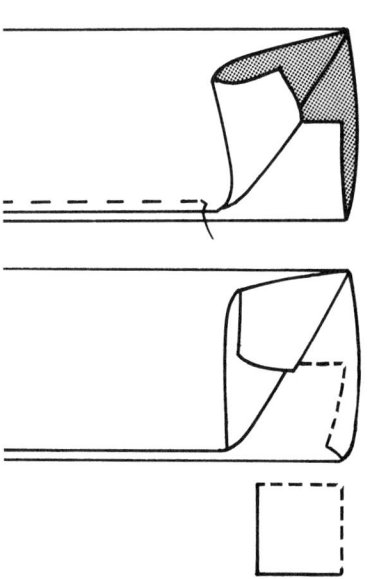

The **closed pocket** is cut in two pieces, with seams allowed all around each and no hem. One piece will be the useful depth of the pocket and the other will be only a 1-inch strip plus seams. Sew a zipper between the two pieces, press all the edges under, using the ½-inch seam allowance, pin in place on the bag, and edgestitch all around.

Handles and **straps** can easily be made of the bag fabric. Cut straight grain strips, twice the finished width, plus two seams (3 inches for a 1-inch finished strap). Add seams to the length also. Fold each edge under on the seam allowance and press. Press the strap wrong sides together so that the folded edges meet. Pin and edgestitch. Edgestitch the opposite side for a finished effect. If the strap or handle is to be stitched on the outside of the bag, press under the seams at the edge and edgestitch at the same time you do the sides. You may wish to trim some of the square of seam out of the corner to prevent bulk.

18 THE BIG BAG BOOK

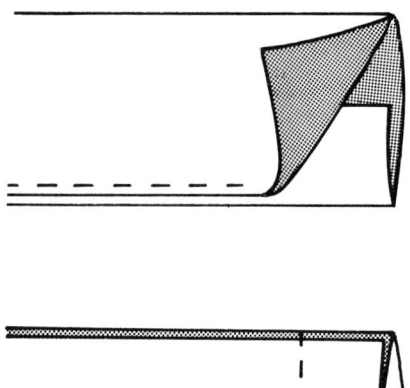

If the fabric is very heavy, **eliminate the seam allowance** along one side by **using the selvage**. Turn the other edge under and proceed as before.

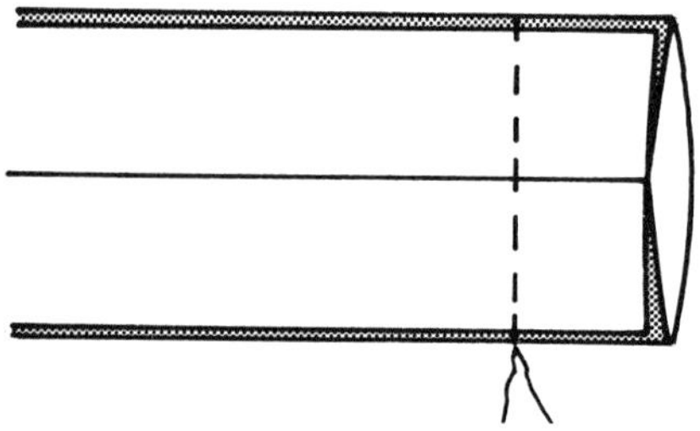

Straps and handles in heavy fabrics can also be seamed and turned in two different ways that reduce bulk. In the first method cut the fabric twice as wide as the finished strap, plus seams. Seam the long side right sides together. Press the seam open and position it exactly in the center —not along the edge—of the unturned strap. Stitch across one end. Trim off the corners and push the stitched end through with the eraser end of a pencil until the strap is right side out. You may leave the strap plain or topstitch the edges.

In the second method cut the fabric as wide as the finished strap, plus seams. Cut another identical piece of the lining fabric. Seam the sides and ends of the fabric piece to the lining piece, leaving an opening of about 3 inches on one long edge. Trim off the corners and push each

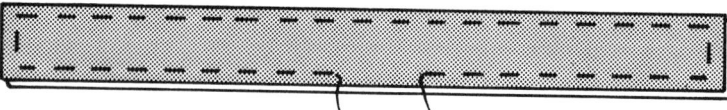

end through the opening. Slipstitch the opening. The nice part about this strap is that you can use a pretty print or contrasting lining to add a touch of color to the outside of the bag.

When stitching the ends of straps or handles to the outside of a bag,

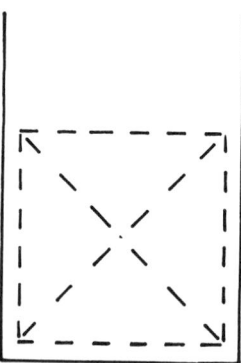

make a square of stitching and then one or two diagonal lines across it for perfect security. When **incorporating handles or straps into a seam,** you can reinforce by backstitching along the seam over the ends of the strap.

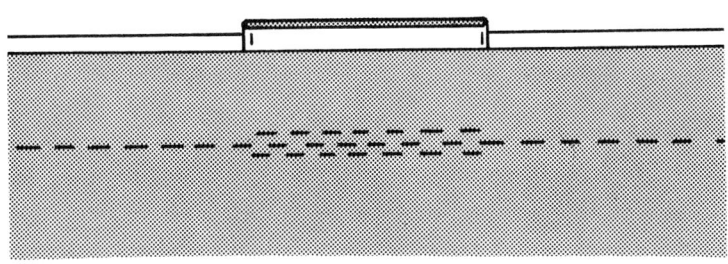

If the ends of straps or handles have not been turned in or seamed and are raw, they can still be applied easily to the outside of a bag. Lay the end of the strap right sides together with the bag in the opposite direction to which it will lie when finished. Seam it onto the bag. Turn the strap up over its seam and proceed as before with a square of stitching.

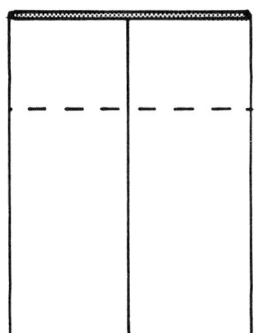

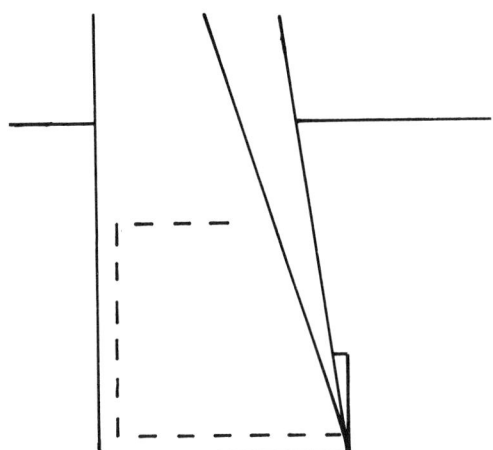

Casings for drawstrings can be made in three ways. The hem of the bag itself can serve as a casing. An unstitched space must be left in one or two seams in the area covered by the hem. It is wise to reinforce such openings with backstitching.

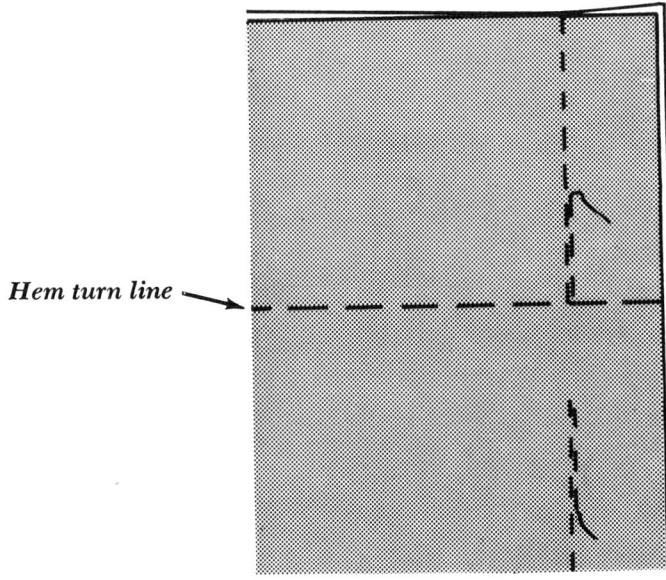

Hem turn line

20 THE BIG BAG BOOK

If you want a **heading** at the top of the bag, make an extra-wide hem and stitch an extra line along it so that the casing is an inch or so below the folded edge. It will again be necessary to leave the opening in the seam.

For heavy fabrics, it may be more practical to finish the edge with a narrow hem, binding, or decorative braid. The **casing can then be**

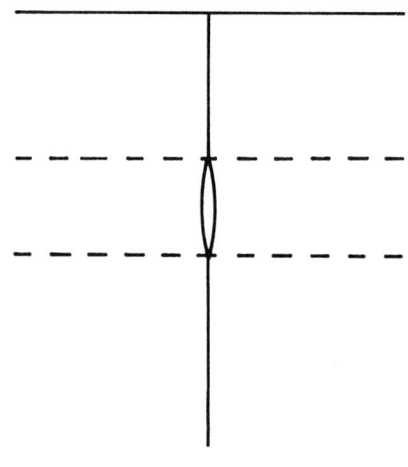
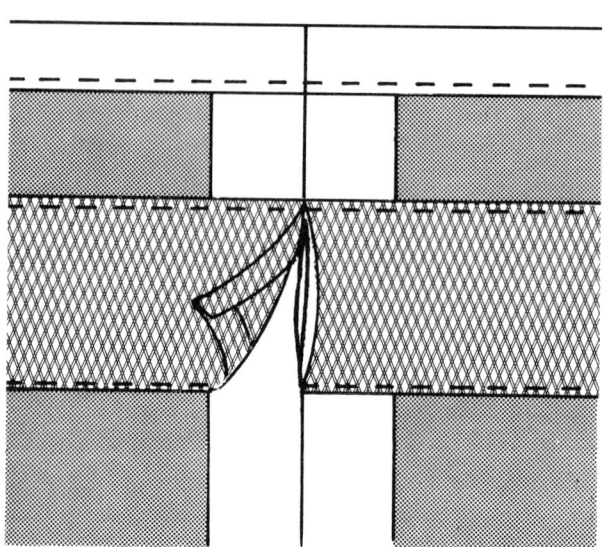

made of 1-inch-wide bias binding—available in packages as quilt binding—below the finished edge. Simply edgestitch it in place inside the bag, again leaving seam openings for the cord.

It should make you happy to know that **zippers** in bags are set in by the two easiest methods imaginable. If you want to shorten a zipper, overcast the teeth firmly at the point where it is to be cut off: read the package. Any zipper, matching or happily contrasting with the color of the bag, can be set in so that it is completely exposed. This is really a matter of seaming the zipper to the two edges of the fabric. You may not

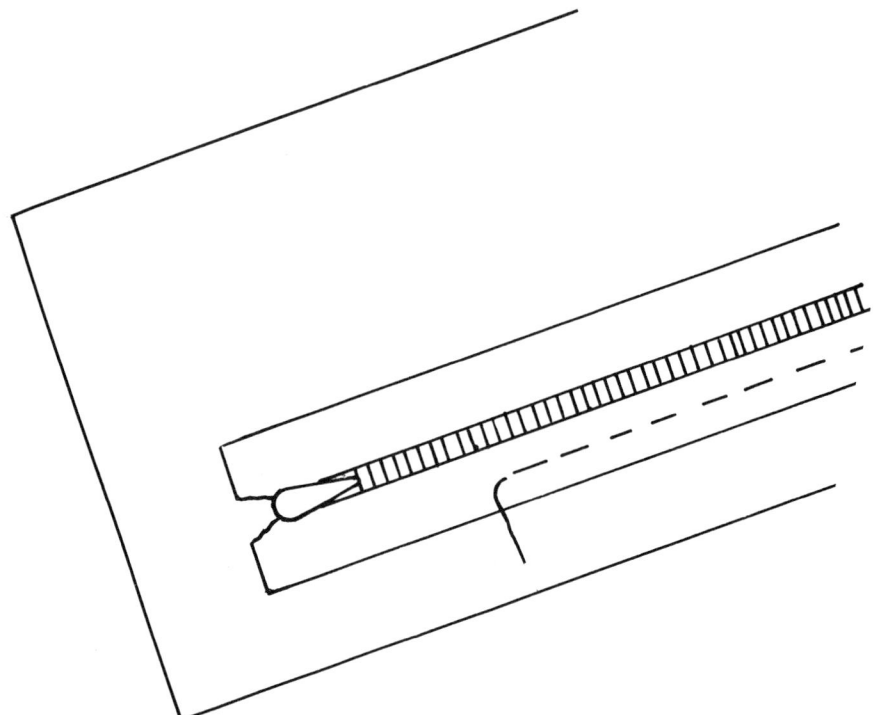

Tricks of the Trade 21

even need to use a zipper foot. Lay the zipper right sides together with the fabric. With the zipper uppermost on your machine, stitch the tape to the seamline, allowing as much of the tape to be exposed as you want. If a very wide section of zipper is to be exposed, you may wish to make a slightly wider seam on the fabric.

Each manufacturer of invisible zippers makes a special machine presser foot to fit his zipper. Use that foot only and the directions that go with that zipper. One practice run may help or use a large machine-basting stitch the first time and, if you get it right, restitch.

There are three basic ways to line a bag easily. If the bag is open at the top, make the lining separately so that when you look down into the bag, everything is neatly finished. The lining will almost always be cut a little shorter than the bag. You may slip it up under the hem, pin the hem firmly in place, and stitch the edge through all layers by machine.

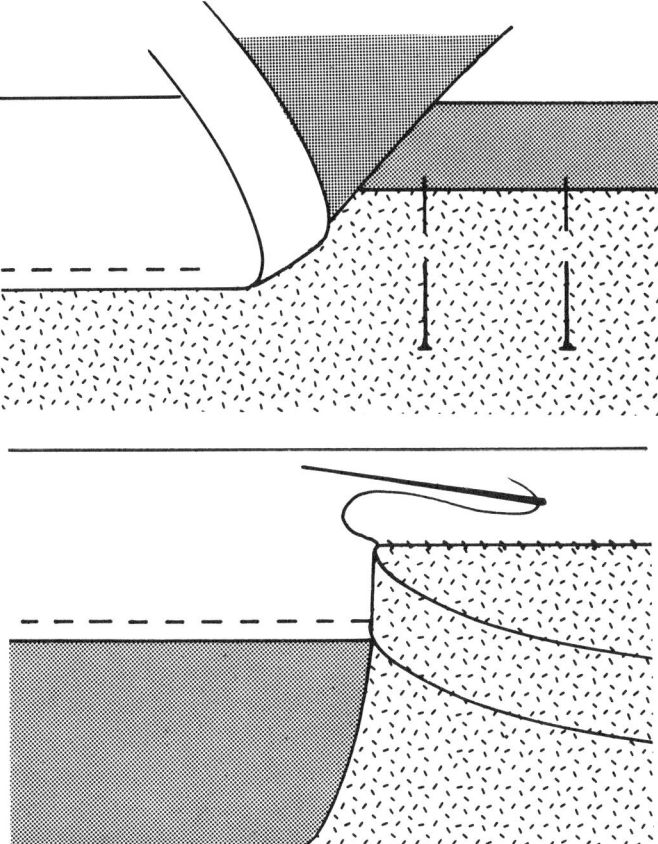

Or you may turn the hem down, stitch it in place, turn under ½ inch along the top of the lining, and slipstitch it in place to the hem.

Bags like the duffle (page 31) or the round boxed bag (page 33) may be lined just as they are interfaced. If an interfacing is to be used, lay it in first, machine baste or fuse it to the outer fabric. Then lay the lining in, wrong sides together, and machine baste it. Continue to assemble the bag pieces with seam or binding. If it is seamed, not bound, you may want to finish the seams.

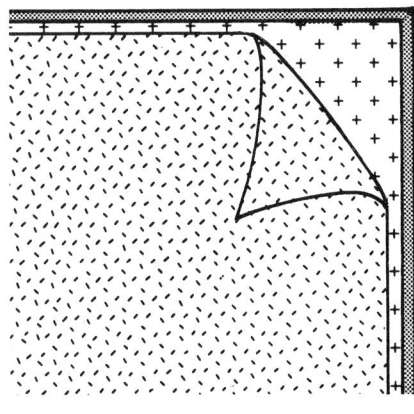

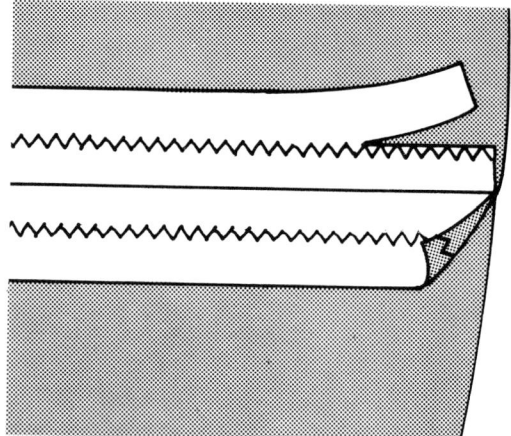

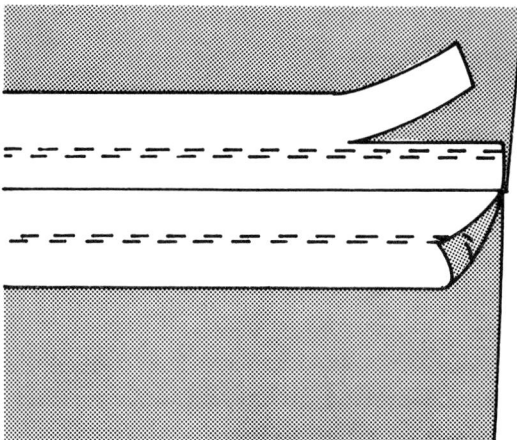

To finish seams run an extra row of stitching, preferably a wide zigzag, about ¼ inch into the seam from the first stitching line and trim the edge of the seam close to the stitching. Cut off the excess seam. On the edge of a hem that is too heavy for the usual ½-inch turn, run a row of wide zigzag stitching or two rows of straight stitching close together. Cut away the excess ½ inch.

Seams can be strengthened with an extra row of machine stitching on the outside, sometimes called a welted seam. After the inside seam is stitched, pinch it together on the outside and stitch through all four layers about ⅛ inch from the edge fold. This is a procedure which should be tested ahead of time, because your machine may rebel at four layers of very heavy fabric.

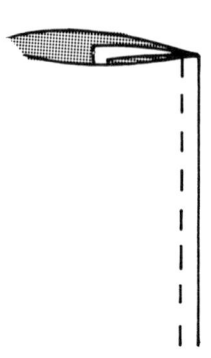

Hand stitching can be done with single or double thread, depending upon how strong you feel it needs to be. Running stitch, backstitch, slipstitch, and blindstitch are the only ones you will need to know.

Many fabrics have an obvious grainline along which you can cut. If the grainline is hard to see, ravel an edge until one thread runs across, or pull a thread out and cut along the opening left. After the grain is straight, you may need to pull the fabric diagonally to square it.

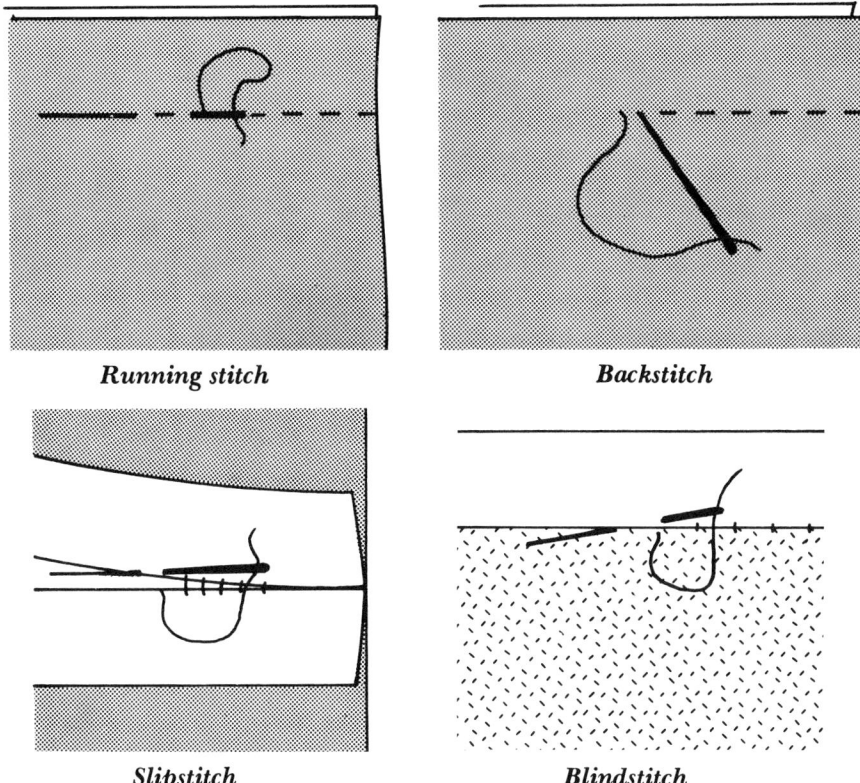

Running stitch *Backstitch*

Slipstitch *Blindstitch*

We found out a few useful things about special fabrics that we will pass on. In very heavy fabrics use the selvage edge as much as possible to prevent intersections too thick to stitch through.

We mentioned earlier that you might need to join synthetic suedes, leathers, and vinyls in some other way than with pins before stitching. Paper clips or transparent tape over the edge or double-sided tape between the seams will do the trick. If you have trouble moving the fabric under the presser foot, try laying a strip of tissue paper along the stitching line so that the foot can slide on it. A special needle for the machine may prevent skipped stitches.

Straw mats, such as we used for the bag on page 149, are quite easy to handle with a medium machine needle, size 14, and a fairly long stitch, 8 or 9 stitches to the inch. Plan carefully and work with care, because straw does not stand up to much stitching and ripping.

Velvets, corduroys, and other napped fabrics must be cut so that the nap runs the same direction on both sides of the bag. This means that even a basic flat bag should have a seam across the bottom. Stitch in the direction that the nap lies so that the seam will creep less than if the machine pushes against the nap. For these fabrics and other delicate ones such as lamé and satin, use a small-to-medium machine needle, size 11 or 14.

If you've never sewed before, start with a simple unlined tote with braid handles. The flat bag with handles at the top, page 26, is easy and can be made without a lining. It might also be a good bag for practicing your first handle and lining. The round bags and boxed bags require a little more skill, but you'll soon work your way up. If you've sewed at all, any bag in this book is within your grasp.

2
Basic Shapes and Things to Come

As we started trying to divide bags into neat categories, more and more shapes and types came to mind and the entire project got completely out of hand. We became bogged down in questions like, "When is a round bag not a round bag?" We decided that the answer might be, "When it is a flat bag or a boxed bag." Very soon even that answer became doubtful and the whole idea more elusive.

After a while we decided that we should be almost completely arbitrary and make the categories fit our fancies. That seemed a little unfair to anyone trying to sort out this problem for information and practicality. So we decided, as always seems the case, on compromise. We made four basic categories and worked the most popular bag shapes into them on the basis of the most similarities in construction. That is why there is a round boxed bag that is not with the round bags. Its construction techniques are more like the boxed-bag techniques. We decided that tote bags—shopping bags made of fabric or leather—are such an important part of today's world that they should have a special category.

The purpose of this chapter is to give some of the techniques that would have to be repeated in the instructions for each bag if the bags were not grouped in this way. Many of the bags in the book are variations on these themes. The exceptions are the bags that are shaped and fitted to certain specific uses. Tote bags actually may be made in several of the other shapes—it is more a matter of size—but the two basic totes given are very quick and easy.

Bags with handles and hardware are in a separate chapter with instructions for their basic shapes. In some cases they overlap the other basics, but they have specific problems of their own.

In all categories we are especially interested in simplicity. Many of the shapes which can be made with zippers can also be made without zippers. There are very easy ways of lining bags and with no handwork. All of the sewing techniques, such as linings, zippers, straps, and seam finishes, are discussed in Chapter 1.

Let's take a quick run-through of what we came up with for basic-shape categories.

1. FLAT

The simplest shape and the nearest to the original concept of a bag is flat. The first bag made was a folded piece of cloth, skin, or woven straw mat, stitched together along two sides. Eventually some also had a flap that folded over to keep the contents in. The clutch purse, the leather briefcase, and the popular Mexican shoulder bag are all bags of this type. If you like to weave or embroider but hate to do intricate forms of sewing, this is your bag! Here we give you three no-nonsense flat bags and later we will explain some highly decorative ones, from tiny to tremendous.

26 THE BIG BAG BOOK

Flat-Bag Construction

Our definition of a flat bag is one that can be made of a continuous piece of fabric, folded and seamed. There is no gusset or inset added to extend the capacity.

The bag can be seamed with a conventional inside seam or joined wrong sides together and bound decoratively on the outside. It can have handles attached to the top or be zipped like a briefcase with a handle at the corner or handles on the side. The clutch purse can be zipped like the briefcase or have a flap.

Pockets can be added inside or outside. Linings are also optional. Unless the fabric is very firm and strong or there is a specific purpose in keeping the bag soft, interfacing is usually a good idea.

If you're using suede, which comes in small pieces, or scraps from something else, you can add a seam at the bottom where we show a fold. You can change our basic dimensions endlessly.

Further along in the book you'll see some variations on flat bags. The shoe carriers and marble or jacks bags are flat bags with drawstrings. There is a great pattern with the handle all in one with the sides in Chapter 14. It's especially attractive for embroidery and decoration.

Flat Bag with Handles

MATERIALS:

If cut lengthwise:
- 1½ yards of any fabric over 18 inches wide
- 1 yard of lining over 18 inches wide
- Interfacing to fit outer fabric

If cut crosswise:
- ⅝ yard of any fabric over 45 inches wide
- ½ yard of lining over 36 inches wide

CUTTING (MEASUREMENTS INCLUDE SEAMS AND HEMS):

After straightening grain, cut outer fabric 40 inches x 17 inches. Cut interfacing 37 inches x 17 inches, lining 33 inches x 17 inches. Cut two handles 15 inches x 2½ inches if on selvage or 3 inches if not.

CONSTRUCTION:

Lay interfacing on wrong side of fabric so that it is 1½ inches short of each end. Fuse or baste it in place. Fold bag right sides together across bottom and stitch side seams. Trim interfacing along seams.

Fold and stitch lining the same way. Cut off lower corners of all seams—press seams open flat. Turn bag right side out, slip lining down inside, and pin top edge in place, 2 inches below raw end of bag.

Turn top edge of bag under ½ inch and then 1 inch for hem and press over lining (page 21). Stitch hem in place.

Fold and stitch handles (page 17). Pin ends of handles on outside of hem, leaving about 6 inches between ends and placing handles on opposite sides. Stitch firmly in place (page 19).

Zip-top Flat Bag (Lady's Briefcase)

MATERIALS:

If cut lengthwise:
   ¾ yard of any fabric over 18 inches wide
   ¾ yard of lining over 18 inches wide
   Interfacing to fit outer fabric
   14-inch neckline zipper (we used contrasting color)
   Optional: soutache braid trim to match zipper
If cut crosswise:
   ½ yard of any fabric over 36 inches wide
   ½ yard of lining over 36 inches wide

CUTTING (MEASUREMENTS INCLUDE SEAMS AND HEMS):

After straightening grain, cut outer fabric, lining, and interfacing pieces 26 inches x 15 inches. Cut small loop handle 7 inches x 2 inches along selvage or make one of ¾-inch ribbon or braid.

CONSTRUCTION:

Lay interfacing on wrong side of fabric and fuse or baste it in place. Stitch zipper in the 15-inch ends by exposed method (page 21). Stitch as many rows of soutache as desired parallel to zipper.

Press and stitch handle (page 18) and fold to form a loop. Seam lining same as bag.

Leave zipper open for turning and seam ends of bag. Incorporate loop handle in one seam just below zipper. Trim interfacing along seams.

Turn bag right side out. Fold top of lining under about ¾ inch and drop lining inside of bag. Hand stitch lining in place along zipper tape (page 21).

Fold-over Flat Clutch

MATERIALS:

Small pieces of fabric and lining left over from other projects may be used as long as they are at least 10 inches x 15 inches after the grain is straightened. We used the lining fabric for the binding, so a few inches more was required, but commercial quilt binding (1-inch width) or fold-braid works as well.

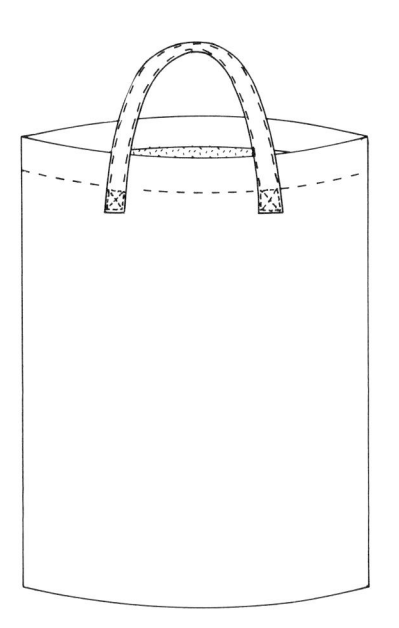

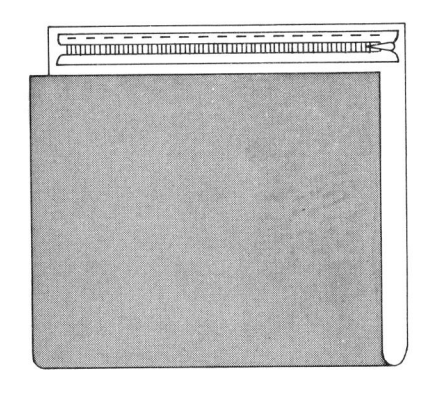

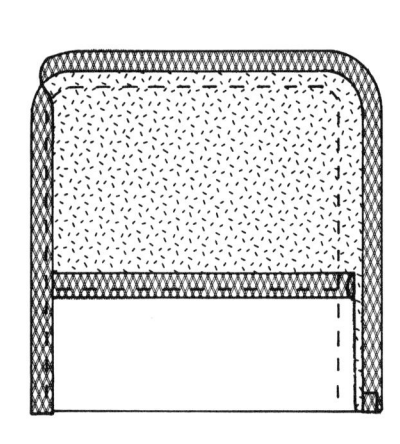

CUTTING (NO SEAM OR HEM NEEDED):

After straightening grain, cut outer fabric, interfacing, and lining 10 inches x 15 inches. Round off corners at one end of all pieces using a compass or dressmaker ruler. Cut 40 inches of 2½-inch-wide bias binding from lining fabric.

CONSTRUCTION:

Lay interfacing on wrong side of fabric and fuse or baste it in place. Lay lining with wrong side against interfacing and baste it in place.

Bind straight end of bag. Fold straight edge up to a depth of 5 inches and pin or baste sides together.

Bind around all raw edges from bottom fold back to bottom fold (page 15).

2. ROUND

The two extremes of round bags are the rather masculine duffle shape and the fat little ladylike drawstring, the direct descendant of a Victorian reticule. They have in common the problem of how to seam a straight piece around a circle. The drawstring is infinitely easier, because there's only one circle and because the other part can be gathered on, leaving a margin for error. The duffle is also one shape that almost demands a zipper.

Round-Bag Construction

There are several techniques which apply to round bags but can also be helpful in the making of boxed bags and side-panel totes. The one big important point is that you must pin and stitch the pieces together exactly on the seamline—½ inch from the edge. In planning the sizes of pieces, remember that 3.14 times the diameter of the circle—from seamline to seamline—is the circumference, or the measurement to which the straight piece must be fitted. Then you may add a little extra length to the straight piece and ease it slightly to the round. Better too much than too little, and the straight piece can be reduced along its straight seam or at the zipper later if you've overdone it.

When the straight piece is to be gathered onto the round, you're free to make it at least half again as long as the circumference of the circle. If you use two lines of gathering—the largest straight stitch on your machine—one on each side of the seamline, you can control the fullness exactly.

Mark the round pieces with four notches spaced evenly, like N., S., E., and W. on the compass. Fold the matching edge of the straight piece and clip it in four spots, equally placed. You will then have four points to pin together first and all the rest should work in between easily. Two little tricks will help. Place the pin across the seamline, picking up only a very small piece of fabric. Clip the straight edge every ½ inch to a depth of about ⅜ inch so that it will relax around the curve.

The soft bag rarely requires stiffening except in the bottom piece and need not be lined in most cases. The duffle, on the other hand, unless made of very stiff fabric like canvas, needs interfacing throughout. We found that the easy all-in-one lining was the perfect answer to finishing the inside with a touch of color and elegance.

Soft, Round Drawstring Bag

MATERIALS:

½ yard of soft pliable fabric over 45 inches wide
Interfacing to fit bottom piece
1 yard of cord for drawstring

CUTTING (MEASUREMENTS INCLUDE SEAMS AND HEMS):

After straightening grain, cut side piece 32 inches x 17 inches. Cut two layers for bottom 7½ inches in diameter (one piece may be of a lighter lining fabric). Cut interfacing identical to bottom.

CONSTRUCTION:

Seam 17-inch ends of side piece right sides together from one end to a point 10½ inches from beginning, leave 1-inch opening for casing, and continue seam to end (page 19). Turn 4½ inches down for hem, finishing edge as desired with ½-inch turn or zigzag. Machine stitch hemline 2 inches from turned top edge and another line for casing 1 inch above that. The two stitching lines should be at each end of the casing opening, forming a casing and heading.

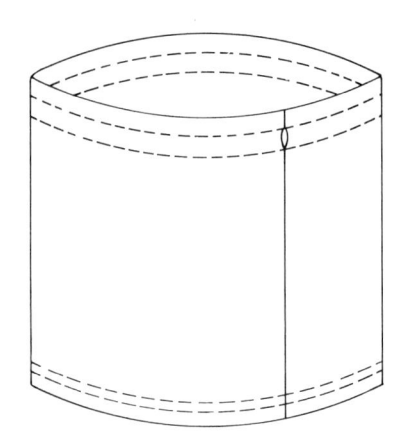

Lay the interfacing on the wrong side of one bottom piece and fuse or baste in place. Lay other bottom piece or lining piece wrong side down on interfacing and baste in place. Gather lower edge of side piece to fit bottom piece along seamline (about 21 inches for circumference of 6½-inch diameter). Distribute gathers evenly and pin edge right sides together around layered bottom piece. Stitch from gathered side, keeping gathers smoothly spaced. Make an extra row of stitching, preferably zigzag, about ¼ inch from raw edge and trim seam. When bag is turned right side out, the long edge of the hem will hang down inside far enough to act as a sort of lining when the bag is open. The cord can be pulled through the casing with a bodkin or safety pin and the ends finished with knots, tassels, or large ornamental buttons.

Small Duffle (Purse or Dolly Duffle)

MATERIALS:

1 yard of any firm fabric over 36 inches wide (slightly less if handles are made of braid or webbing)
½ yard of any lightweight lining fabric over 36 inches wide
Interfacing same as lining
1¾ yards of 1-inch-wide braid or webbing for handles—optional
12-inch zipper (invisible is good)

CUTTING (MEASUREMENTS INCLUDE SEAMS AND HEMS):

After straightening grain, cut side rectangle 22 inches x 14 inches. Cut two round end pieces 7½ inches in diameter. Cut interfacing and lining pieces identical to outer pieces. If desired, cut fabric handles 3 inches x 58 inches (may be pieced) and pocket 6 inches x 7 inches.

CONSTRUCTION:

Lay interfacing on wrong side of each piece and fuse or baste it in place. Baste lining wrong side down to interfacing on end pieces only.

Fold and stitch handles so that they are 1 inch wide with unfinished ends (page 19). Form a smooth, untwisted circle of handles and join raw ends with zigzag or hand stitching so that they meet but do not overlap. Mark the point opposite joining. Fold the bag rectangle across to determine the center bottom. Lay handles 7 inches apart with marked points at center bottom line. Stitch each handle down firmly along its edges to a point within 3 inches of the ends of rectangle.

Make up pocket (page 17), and stitch in place between handles on one side.

Lay lining wrong side down to interfacing of rectangle and baste or stitch together around edges. Sew zipper into ends, thus joining rectangle into a tube. Finish zipper seam with zigzag to prevent fraying. Leave zipper open for turning bag after the ends are joined.

Pin each open end of rectangle to one of the circular pieces and stitch seam (page 29). Stitch again at ¼ inch from raw edge—preferably with zigzag—and trim seam. Turn bag right side out through zipper.

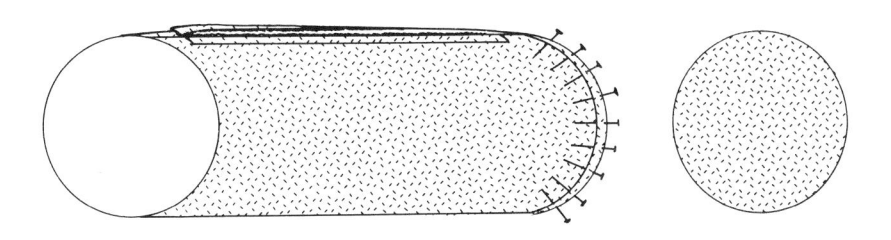

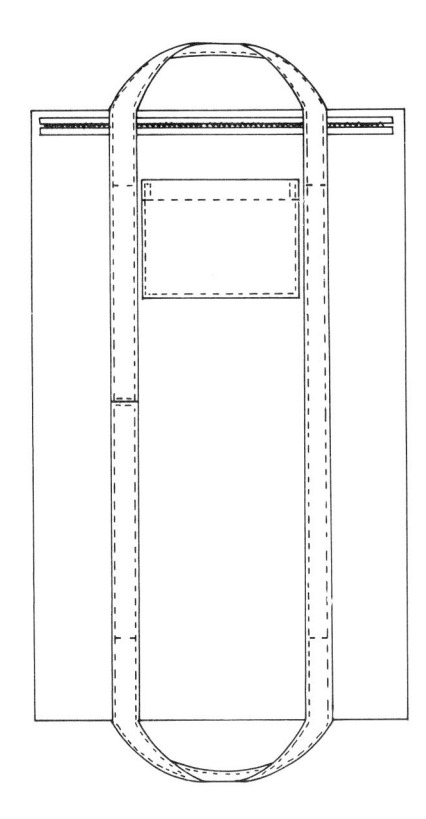

3. BOXED

A bag that has a strip around the sides, adding greatly to its capacity, is described as boxed, just like its close cousin, the boxed pillow. The technique for making it is almost exactly like making a decorative pillow cover. It can be simplified by leaving out the zipper, and, of course, it needs handles. The shape lends itself to decoration with outside bound seams or piped seams.

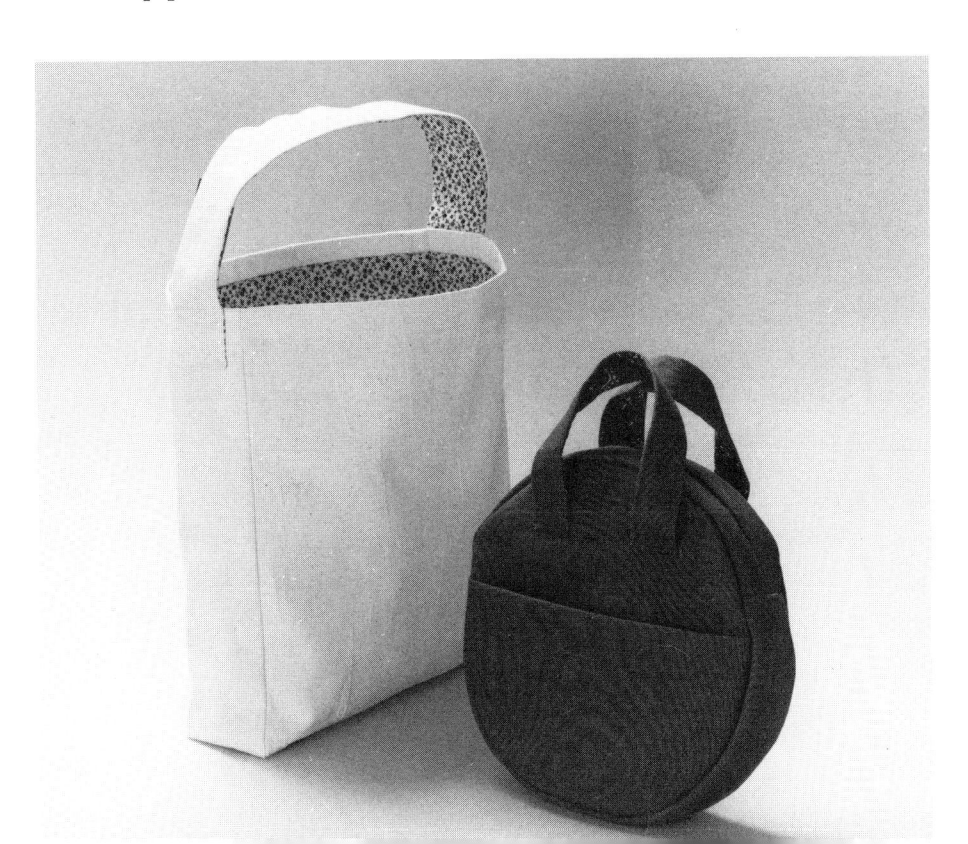

32 THE BIG BAG BOOK

Boxed-Bag Construction

Both round boxed bags and square or rectangular boxed bags have some construction features very much like round bags. Careful measuring, marking, and clipping at the turn make them go together smoothly. Again, remember that measurements must be the same on the seamlines, not on the cut edges.

A zipper can be set into a section of the boxing strip, exactly the way it is in a pillow. On the other hand, the top can be left open as on a tote bag. Many variations can be made on the handles and closures, as you will see later in the book.

Standard Boxed Carry-all

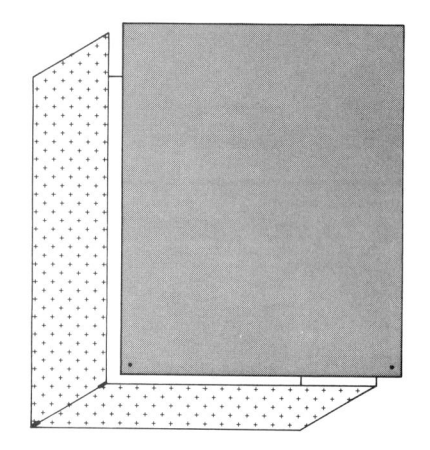

MATERIALS:

¾ yard of any fabric over 45 inches wide
¾ yard of any lining fabric over 45 inches wide
Interfacing for boxing strip or for entire bag, as desired

CUTTING (MEASUREMENTS INCLUDE SEAMS AND HEMS):

After straightening grain, cut two side rectangles 16 inches x 13 inches. Cut a boxing strip 4 inches x 43 inches. Cut a handle 3 inches x 20 inches. Cut lining pieces 13 inches x 13 inches, 4 inches x 40 inches, and 3 inches x 20 inches. Cut interfacing for boxing strip and for other pieces, if desired.

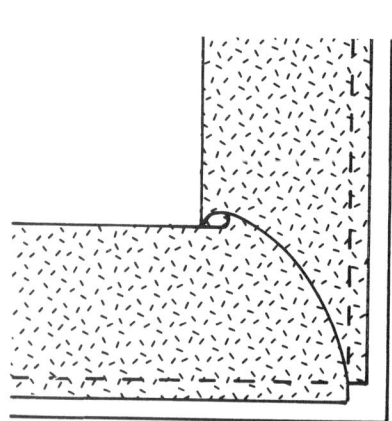

CONSTRUCTION:

Lay interfacing on wrong side of boxing strip, and any other pieces desired, and fuse or baste it in place. Mark exact center of both sides of boxing strip and of one short side of each side rectangle. Start pinning boxing strip right sides together with side rectangles at these points. At corner clip boxing strip almost ½ inch deep so that it will turn corner and continue up sides. Stitch both seams, press, and turn bag right side out.

Turn top hem under 1½ inches and stitch. Seam handle and handle lining together (page 18), and turn. Stitch each end in place at top of boxing strip.

Make up lining same as outside, without handle. Turn upper edge of lining under and attach by hand to inside of bag hem.

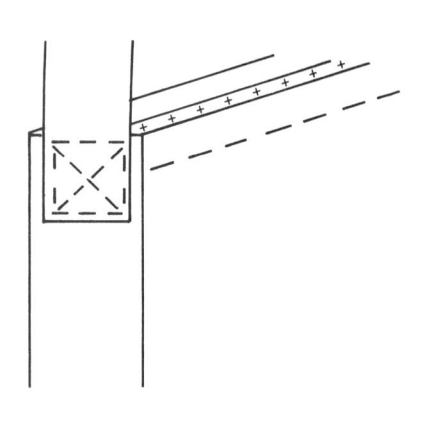

Round Boxed Purse

MATERIALS:

⅝ yard of any firm fabric over 36 inches wide
⅝ yard of any lightweight lining fabric over 36 inches wide
Interfacing to fit outer fabric
12-inch zipper (invisible is good)

Basic Shapes and Things to Come   33

CUTTING (MEASUREMENTS INCLUDE SEAMS AND HEMS):

After straightening grain, cut two round sides 11 inches in diameter. Cut one boxing strip 3½ inches x 21 inches and two zipper-area strips 2¼ inches x 13 inches. Cut two handles 2¼ inches x 16 inches. If desired, cut a pocket piece a little more than half of one of the round sides, about 7 inches deep, with a straight upper edge. Cut lining identical to every piece, including handles and pocket. Cut interfacing for any pieces desired—probably omitting pocket.

CONSTRUCTION:

Lay interfacing on wrong side of each piece and fuse or baste it in place. Lay lining wrong side down to interfacing of all pieces except handles and pocket and baste in place.

Sew zipper between two narrow strips and finish seam edges with zigzag stitching to prevent raveling along zipper. Sew ends of zipper strip to ends of other boxing strip.

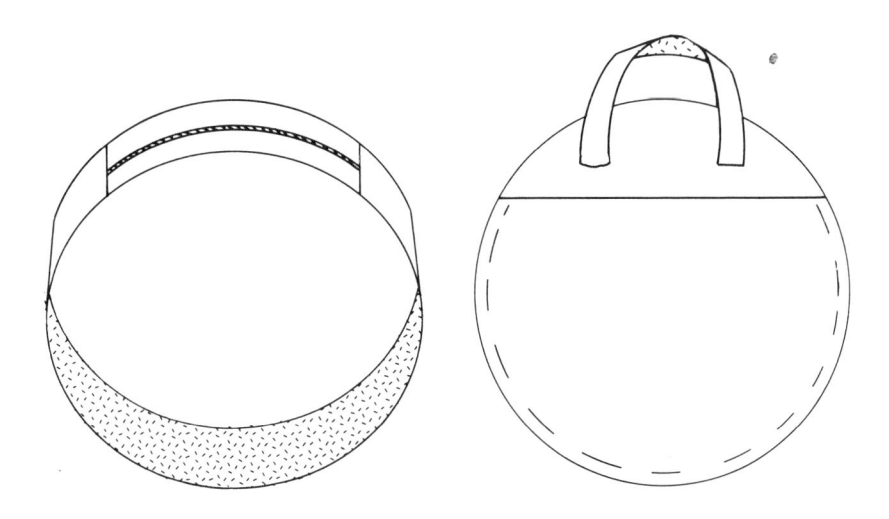

Line handles with lining and turn (page 18). Sew handles to form loops near the upper edge of each round side piece.

Face upper straight edge of pocket with lining piece and baste pocket flat to one side at lower edge.

Pin and stitch boxing strip in place between two round sides (page 29). Be sure to leave zipper open so that bag can be turned right side out. Stitch seams again about ¼ inch from edge, trim, and turn bag.

4. TOTES

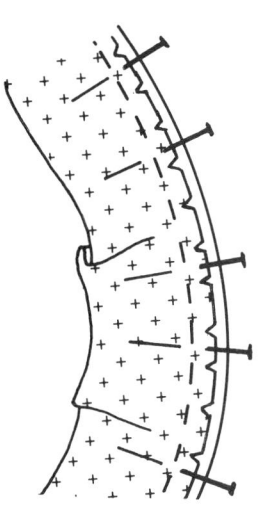

Actually it's hard to say whether a tote bag is defined by its shape or its size. The origin of the tote bag must have been the shopping bag, one of the great inventions of this era of no-delivery supermarkets and mile-wide shopping-center lots! The competition among businesses in decorating these has made simple advertisements into an art form. The dedicated bag maker should follow suit and decorate—with monograms, appliqués, fabric paint.

Tote-Bag Construction

The simplest and greatest of all tote bags is truly like a shopping bag, made in one straight strip folded and seamed together up the sides. Up to that point it is just like the first flat bag we mentioned, but then comes the big difference. The two lower corners are folded back on themselves and mitered across, forming a square lower section. At its most utilitarian it also has those marvelous wraparound straps that support great amounts of weight.

We have included another type of tote, which is a cross between the real tote and the rectangular boxed bag. It has side panels that may or may not be rounded at the bottom. It lends itself nicely to certain outside seaming and decoration.

Mitered Corner Tote

MATERIALS:

1¼ yards of any fabric over 45 inches wide will make two identical bags if braid or webbing is used for the handles.

1⅛ yards of any light lining fabric over 45 inches wide will line both bags.

3 yards of strong braid or webbing, 1 inch or 2 inches wide, will make handles for each bag.

CUTTING (MEASUREMENTS INCLUDE SEAMS AND HEMS):

After straightening fabric, cut bag piece 41 inches x 22 inches. Cut lining 37 inches x 22 inches.

CONSTRUCTION:

Fold the bag piece across the shortest way to determine a center line—the center bottom of the bag—and mark this with chalk or basting. Mark two points on this line 7 inches apart and centered as placement for the handles.

Form a circle with the handle webbing and join the raw ends, making sure that there is no twist. Mark the point opposite the joining and place it and the joining on the marked points at the bottom of the bag, so that the inner edges are 7 inches apart. Align the straps evenly with the edge of the bag, pin in place, and stitch. Stop stitching about 4 inches below upper edge of bag.

Pin and stitch side seams. Press seams open flat. With bag wrong side out, lay seam down on marked center bottom line, forming a right-angle corner. With a ruler draw a line perpendicular to the seam across the corner at a point where the length will be 5 inches—2½ inches on each side of the seam. Stitch across this line, backstitching at each end for security.

When both corners are finished with this triangular miter, they may be cut off ½ inch from the stitching, like any other seam, or left in place to make the bottom of the bag firmer.

Turn the top of the bag under 1½ inches and hem. Make lining like bag, slip inside bag, and turn under along upper edge and hand stitch in place to the hem.

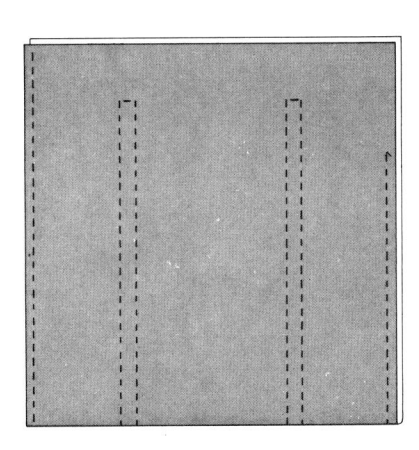

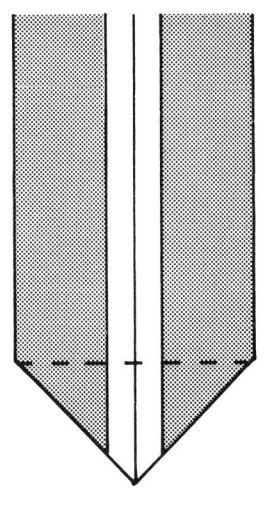

Side Panel Tote

MATERIALS:

1¼ yards of any firm fabric over 36 inches wide
1⅛ yards of any light lining fabric over 36 inches wide
Interfacing for side panels and other pieces as desired

CUTTING (MEASUREMENTS INCLUDE SEAMS AND HEMS):

After straightening grain, cut one rectangle 41 inches x 18 inches. Cut two side panels 4 inches x 20 inches and round off one end. Cut two handles 3½ inches x 27 inches. Cut rectangle of lining 37 inches x 18 inches and two side panels of lining 4 inches x 18 inches.

CONSTRUCTION:

Lay interfacing on wrong side of side panels, and any other pieces desired, and fuse or baste in place. Mark center bottom of rectangle by folding across as on previous tote. Mark center of bottom end of each side panel. Starting from these marked points, pin panels into sides. Depending upon how much you rounded the ends, the rectangle may be a little long for the side panels but can be trimmed off to match. Review boxing strips (page 32) for ways of making seaming easier. Stitch seams. Stitch again ¼ inch from edge and trim.

Fold handles, press, and stitch (page 18). Turn under upper edge of bag 1½ inches and stitch hem. Join handles in a loop on each side at top of bag and stitch in place.

Mark, pin, and seam lining together in the same way as outer bag. Slip it inside of bag, turn top edge under, and hand stitch in place.

Remember that the instructions in this section are only the most basic ones—for the bags in the sizes shown. Added pockets, more detailed zipper directions, ways to construct handles of fabric, and so on, are in the section on sewing details. The alphabet and directions for using it to monogram the bags will be found on pages 123–124. There are embroidery suggestions and other ways to decorate all through the book. Tote bags are so important that there is a special chapter devoted to them. The real fun of making bags is not to copy a pattern exactly but to take the ideas presented and mix and match to create a personal statement.

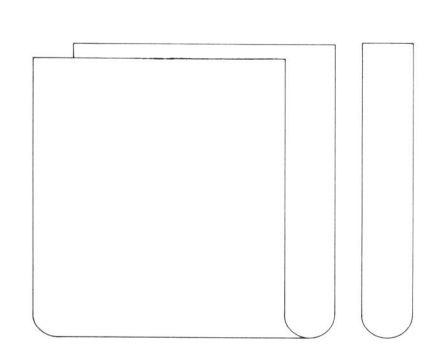

3

The Great Easy Tote Bag

The tote bag can be made in every size, weight, and texture imaginable. A large canvas one can be used for carrying boat equipment, ski boots, clothes for a casual weekend, or anything that man, woman, or child can lift to tote. It can also be made very small, in velvet or satin or gold synthetic leather for carrying a lipstick and some mad money. It can be made wide, tall, square, with or without lining, with or without pockets, and with or without decoration.

The most basic tote bag is simply a rectangle of fabric, seamed up the sides, mitered at the two lower corners, and hemmed. Straps of braid or webbing or fabric can be sewed on all the way around while the bag is still flat, or shorter ones can be added at the top when it is finished.

We have also included a panel-sided tote, which is a cross between a basic tote and a boxed rectangular bag. In this chapter we include several of both kinds in an assortment of shapes and fabrics and with all sorts of pockets and closures. See plate 1 for a color picture of the collection and page 33 for basic instructions.

1. The big bag at the bottom left of the ladder is made exactly by the basic-tote-shape directions on page 34 and the monogram is from instructions on page 128. It is faded tan denim, backed with medium-weight Pellon® and lined with a brown calico print. The red-orange tote on the cover is made in the same size in a firm canvas, unlined.

2. The green monogrammed bag just above the tan one on the ladder is made by the side-panel tote directions on page 36. It is in the same weight of faded denim as the tan one, with lining and monogram of multitoned green cotton print. Monogram directions are on page 122. The handles are of self-fabric, keeping cost to a minimum.

3. The huge leather-look bag with the zipper top, at the bottom center of the ladder, came into being because a friend had some marvelous wall-covering material left over. It has a suede finish and a firm fabric backing. We tested it on the machine and found that it could be

38 THE BIG BAG BOOK

sewed with a heavy needle by the instructions for synthetic leathers in Chapter 1. Here are step-by-step instructions for this type of bag.

Leather-look Tote with Zipper Top (four steps)

a. Cut a rectangle of fabric, 23 inches x 40 inches, and two insets, 3½ inches x 19½ inches. You will need 3 yards of jute trim and 1½ yards of beige grosgrain in a matching width for the handles, and an 18-inch separating zipper. Sew the jute trim on for handles, stopping the stitching 5 inches from each end of the bag. Center the insets, as shown, at each end and seam them in place, stopping and backstitching ¾ inch from the ends.

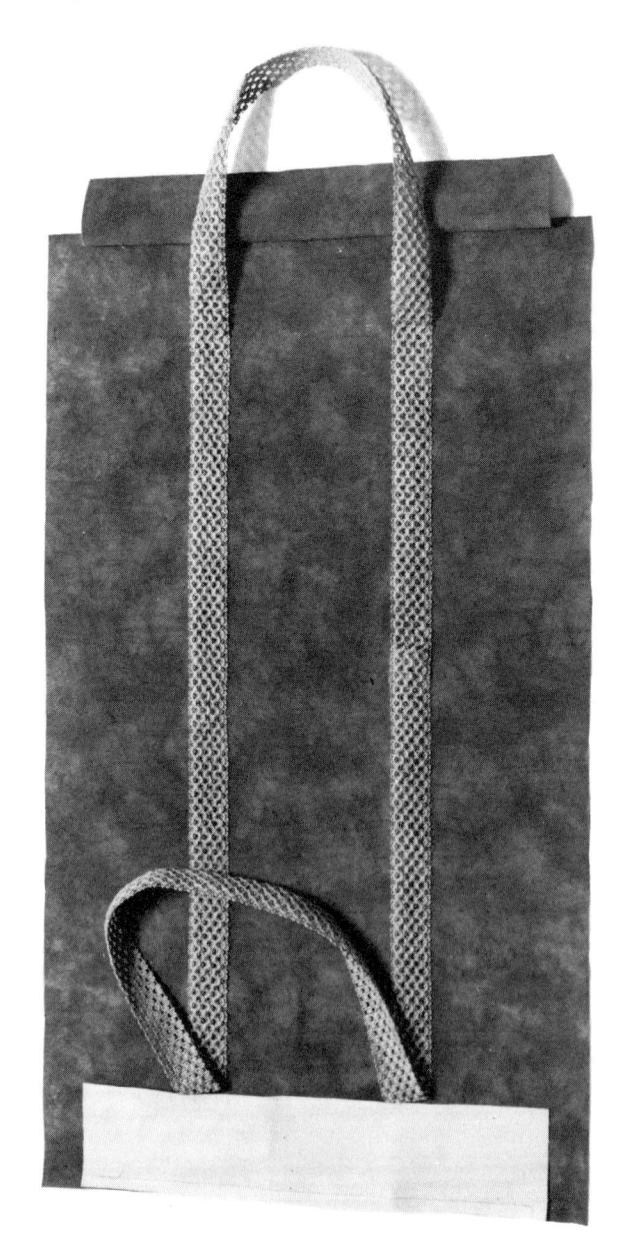

The Great Easy Tote Bag 39

b. Sew the zipper between the insets, leaving an equal amount of fabric at each end to be hemmed narrowly. Edgestitch the ribbon on the back of the free part of each handle. Stitch the handles, including the ribbon, 1 inch farther toward the ends of the bag.

c. Seam the sides as for any basic tote. Miter the corners 5 inches across—but on the outside of the bag. Turn under the ends of the insets about ½ inch and machine hem. The hem should cover the ends of the zipper and hold the zipper firmly in position.

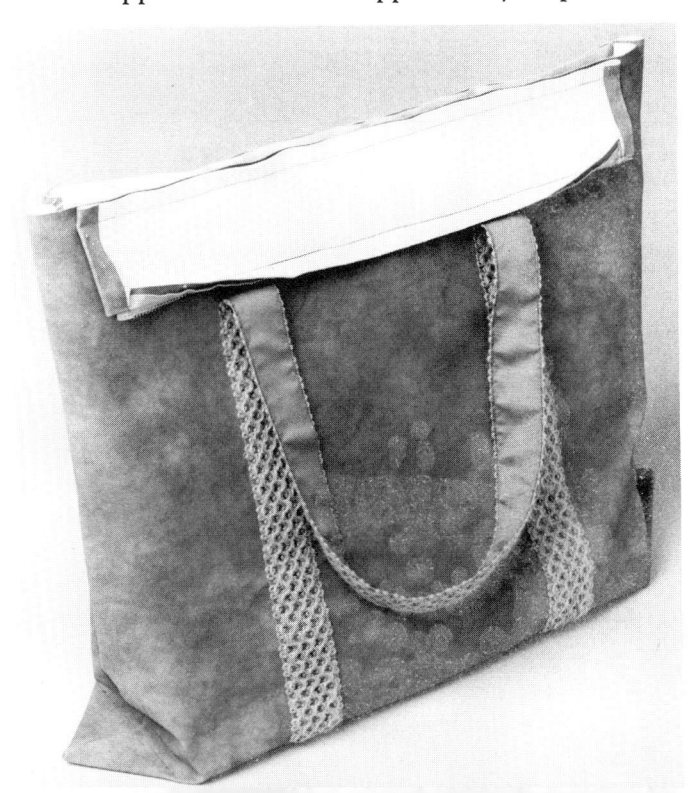

d. Unzip the zipper until it lies completely open. Turn the top down 1½ inches for a hem. Holding the handles and the zipper insets out of the way, machine hem the bag 1 inch down from the folded edge. You should be stitching through the seamlines of the insets. Hand tack the mitered corners up against the side seams. See page 39.

4. If you're the kind of person who tries to put more into a bag than it was ever meant to hold, you're just like the rest of the human race. The tote bag second from the bottom on the right of the ladder was designed to take care of this age-old problem. The soft drawstring extension lets you keep on stuffing things in just as far as the handles will allow. Here's how we did it.

a. Cut a rectangle of printed denim 36 inches x 16 inches and a matching interfacing. We used a fusible Pellon® for extra strength and stiffness because the denim was a fashion weight. Cut a lining 32 inches x 16 inches, and two top extension pieces 12 inches x 16 inches, both of matching lightweight cotton or cotton blend. Cut handles 90 inches x 3½ inches—pieced if necessary—and a 36-inch piece of medium-weight cable cord.

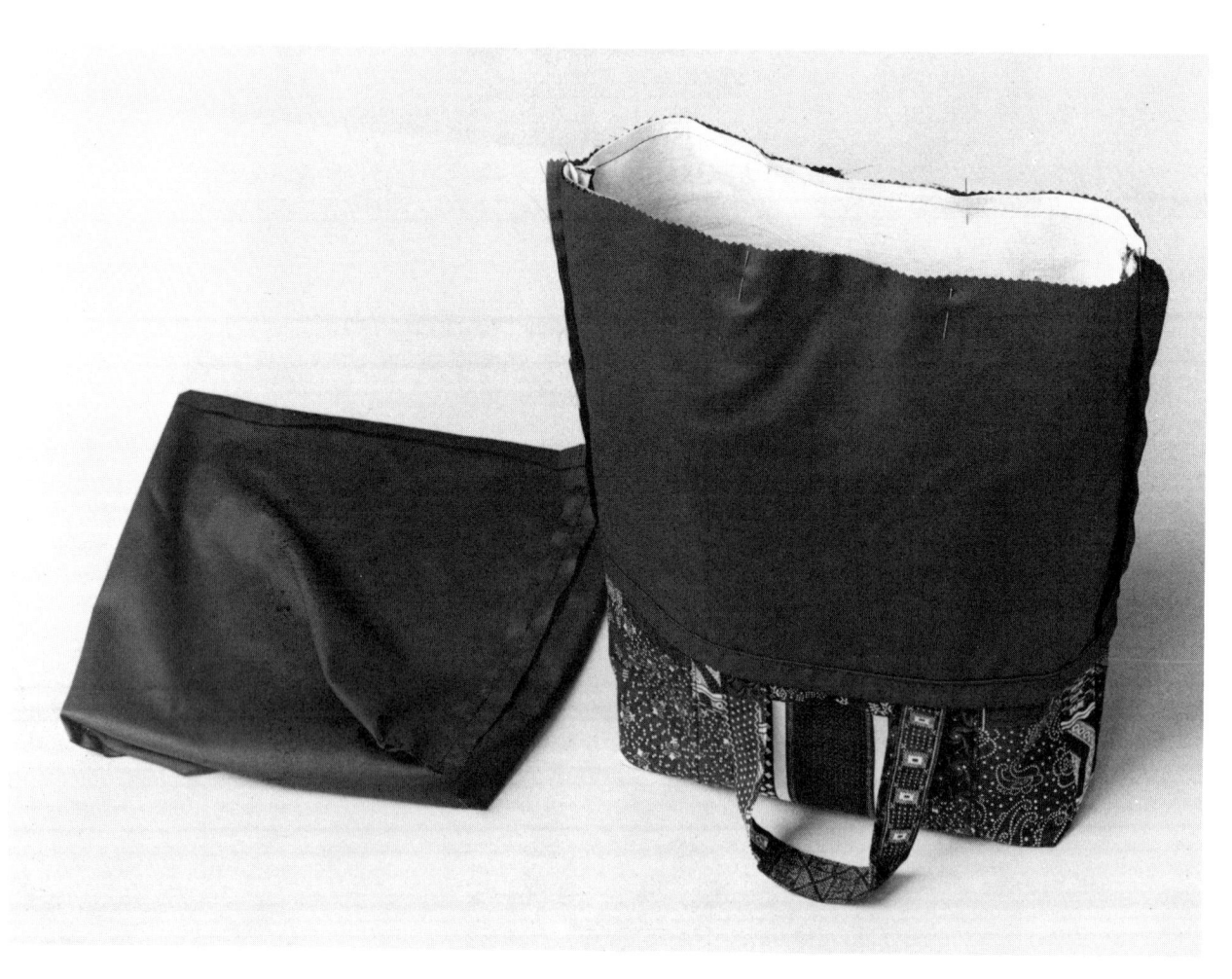

Fuse the interfacing to the wrong side of the rectangle. Make up the handles (page 17), and apply as for the basic tote bag (page 35). After the side seams are sewed and pressed, miter the bottom corners 4 inches across. Make the lining to fit. Seam the 12-inch ends of the top extension pieces to form a tube, leave a ¾-inch opening 1¼ inches from one end for the drawstring. Turn under ¼ inch and then 1 inch, press, and hem for a casing. Seam the other edge of the top extension to the top of the bag, as shown.

b. Turn down the top of the bag itself for a 1½-inch hem. Machine hem it, stitching right along the seamline that holds the top extension to the bag. This pushes the extension down inside and secures it firmly to the bag, leaving a 1-inch doubled hem above it. When

42   THE BIG BAG BOOK

the extension is not in use, it drops comfortably into the bag. Run the cable cord into the casing so that you can pull the top tightly together when you overstuff your tote. Turn the top edge of the lining under ½ inch, drop it inside the bag, and stitch it in place by hand.

5. The big canvas tote at the lower right of the ladder was planned without wraparound handles to allow a large unbroken surface for decoration—see the quilted designs, Chapter 14. We used a rectangle of canvas 23 inches x 37 inches, and 2½ yards of heavy webbing.

a. Make the bag exactly like the basic tote, but without handles. Cut two pieces of webbing 22 inches long for the handles and use the remaining pieces to trim the upper edge of the bag.

b. Pin the handles in place, wrong side to wrong side with the upper edge of the bag, about 8 inches apart. Stitch several times across the ends of the webbing, ½ inch from the raw edge. Lay the long piece of webbing wrong side down to the wrong side of the bag, covering the ends of the handles as far down as the stitching. Edge-stitch the webbing in place all around the top of the bag. The ends of the webbing should overlap and be stitched together. Turn the webbing to the outside of the bag and stitch the other edge down. We used zigzag stitching for extra strength.

6 & 7. The tall and the short totes are shown in the upper-right-hand corner. They are alike except for the dimensions. The tall one holds long things, like loaves of French bread and your favorite tall leather boots. The short one is wonderfully inexpensive and can even serve as a summer purse. The tall one is lightweight canvas, interfaced with fusible Pellon® and lined with a pretty brown calico print. The short one is burlap, interfaced with heavy Pellon®, and lined with a cheery red calico print. The handles are made of the same print—less expensive than webbing. Check the basic tote, Chapter 2, for exact directions.

For the tall tote, cut the fabric and interfacing 13½ inches x 45 inches, the lining 13½ inches x 41 inches, and use 3 yards of corded cotton braid (woven to look like macramé) for the handles. The miter on the lower corner is 3½ inches.

Cut the fabric and the interfacing for the short tote 16 inches x 22 inches, the lining 16 inches x 22 inches, and the handles 3 inches x 72 inches (pieced as necessary). The handles are folded and stitched (page 17) so that they are 1 inch wide finished. The miter on the lower corner is 3½ inches and folded to the outside for strength and decorative effect.

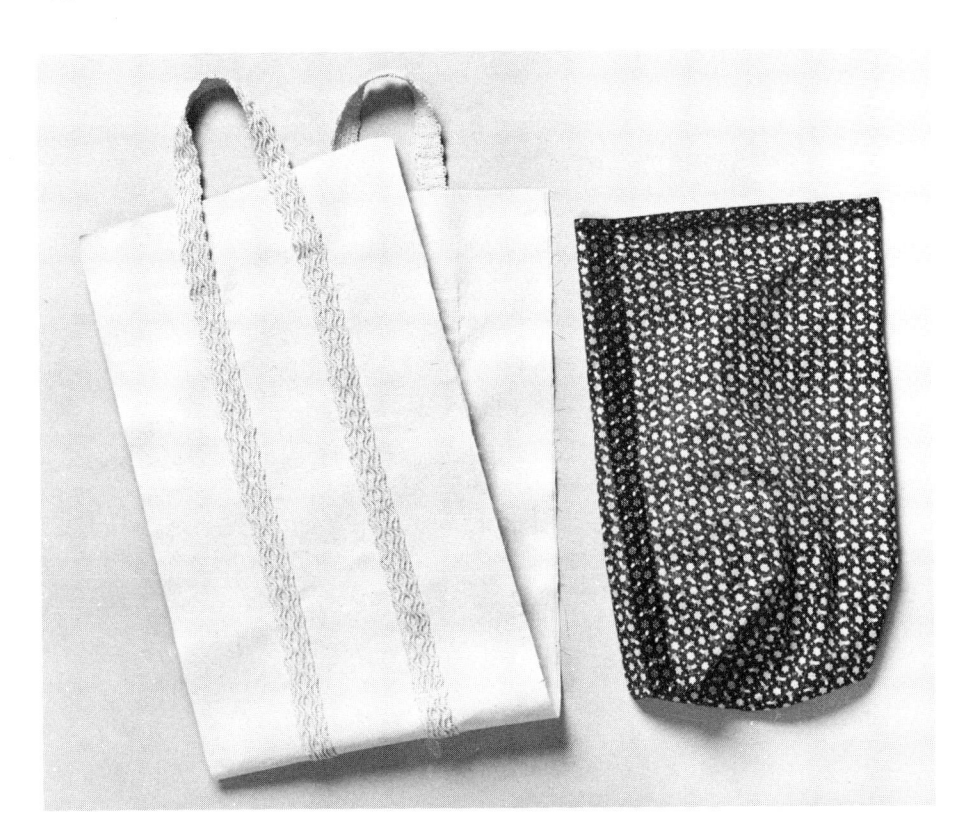

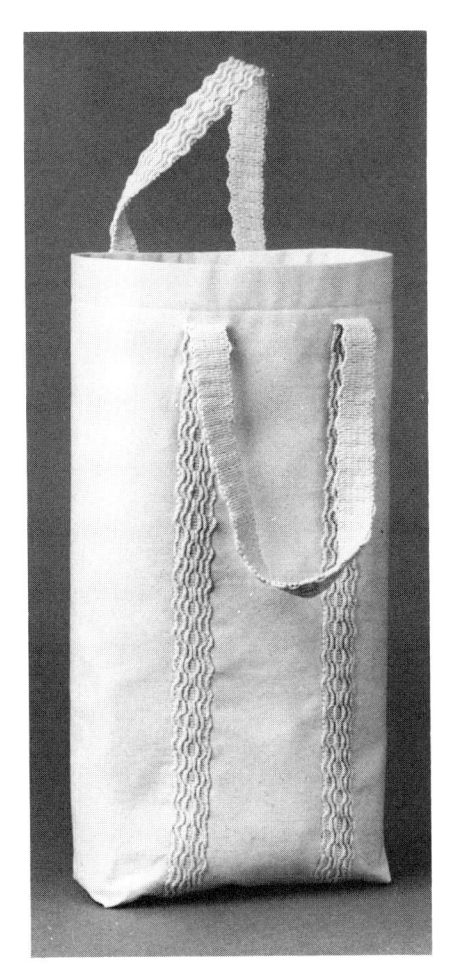

44 THE BIG BAG BOOK

8. The traveling tote at the upper left of the ladder provides zip-tight pockets for all the things that slip down and hide in the bottom of a conventional purse, such as passports, tickets, foreign currency, and whatever you need instantly.

a. Cut a rectangle of canvas 37 inches x 18½ inches, the bottom pocket 8½ inches x 15 inches, and four pockets 8½ inches x 5¼ inches. Seam a 7-inch zipper to one edge of each of the small pockets and to both edges of the large double pocket. We used six different colored zippers for decoration. If you use ½ inch for the seam and let ½ inch of each zipper show, the pockets will work out to the right length to cover the entire length of the bag up to the 1-inch-wide webbing used at the top.

Lay the large pocket at the exact center of the bag rectangle and machine stitch two lines across, 3 inches apart, at the base of the bag (the lines of stitching should be 14 inches from each end of the bag). Seam the bottom of the next pockets right sides together over the zippers on the large double pocket, as shown, stitching through to the bag. After each pocket is sewed on, it will be folded up flat against the bag and another pocket sewed through the upper edge of the zipper.

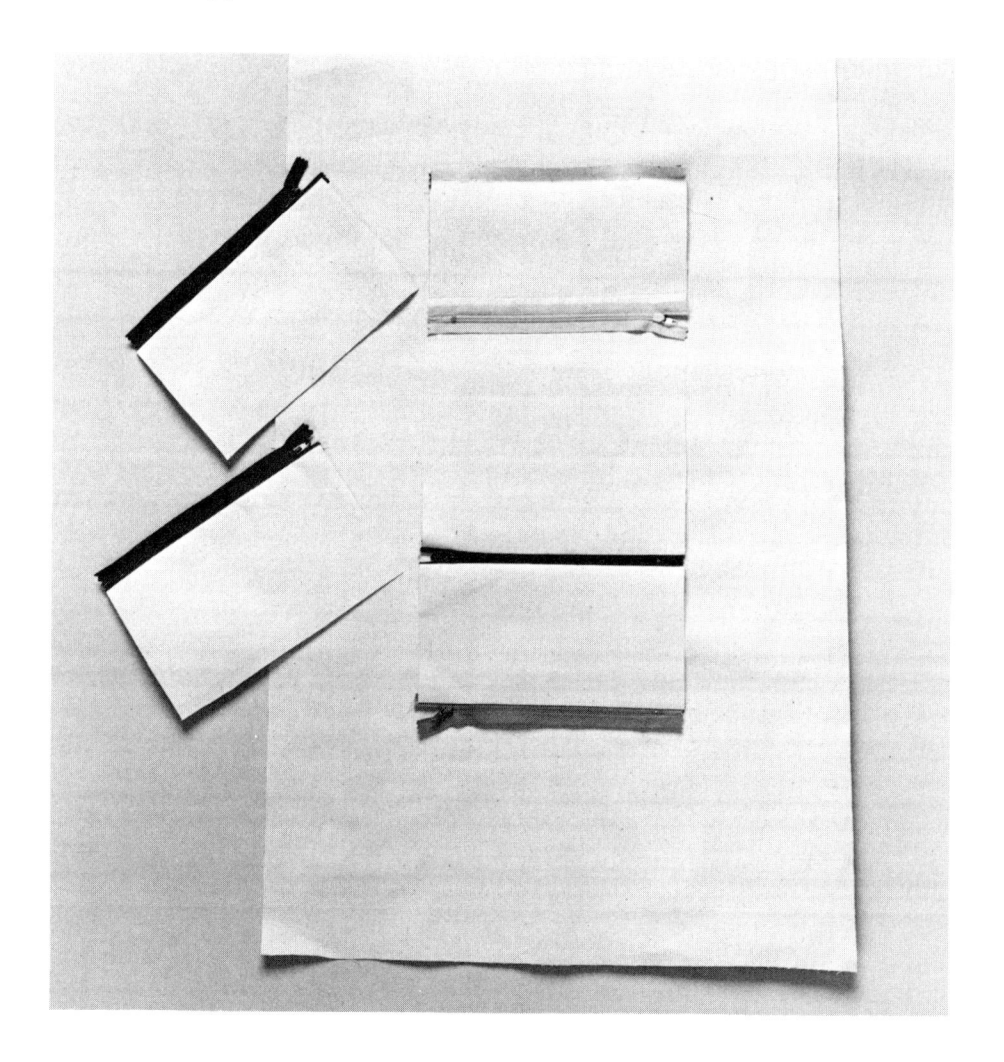

b. You'll need 4 yards of 1-inch-wide webbing, 1 yard to go around the upper edge, and 3 yards for the wraparound handles. Sew the handles in place, covering the raw ends of the pockets, and stop the stitching 2 inches from the ends of the bag rectangles. Finish the sides like the basic tote (page 35), mitering the corners 3½ inches. Use the other yard of webbing to finish the upper edge like the tote described in number 5 above, being sure to bring the webbing down over the upper edge of the last zippers.

9. For those who feel that purses are passé, the city tote just to the lower right of the traveler's tote is a nice replacement. It has an assortment of outside easy-access pockets and pretty trimming to dress it up. Our version is made as a side-panel tote with bound outside seams.

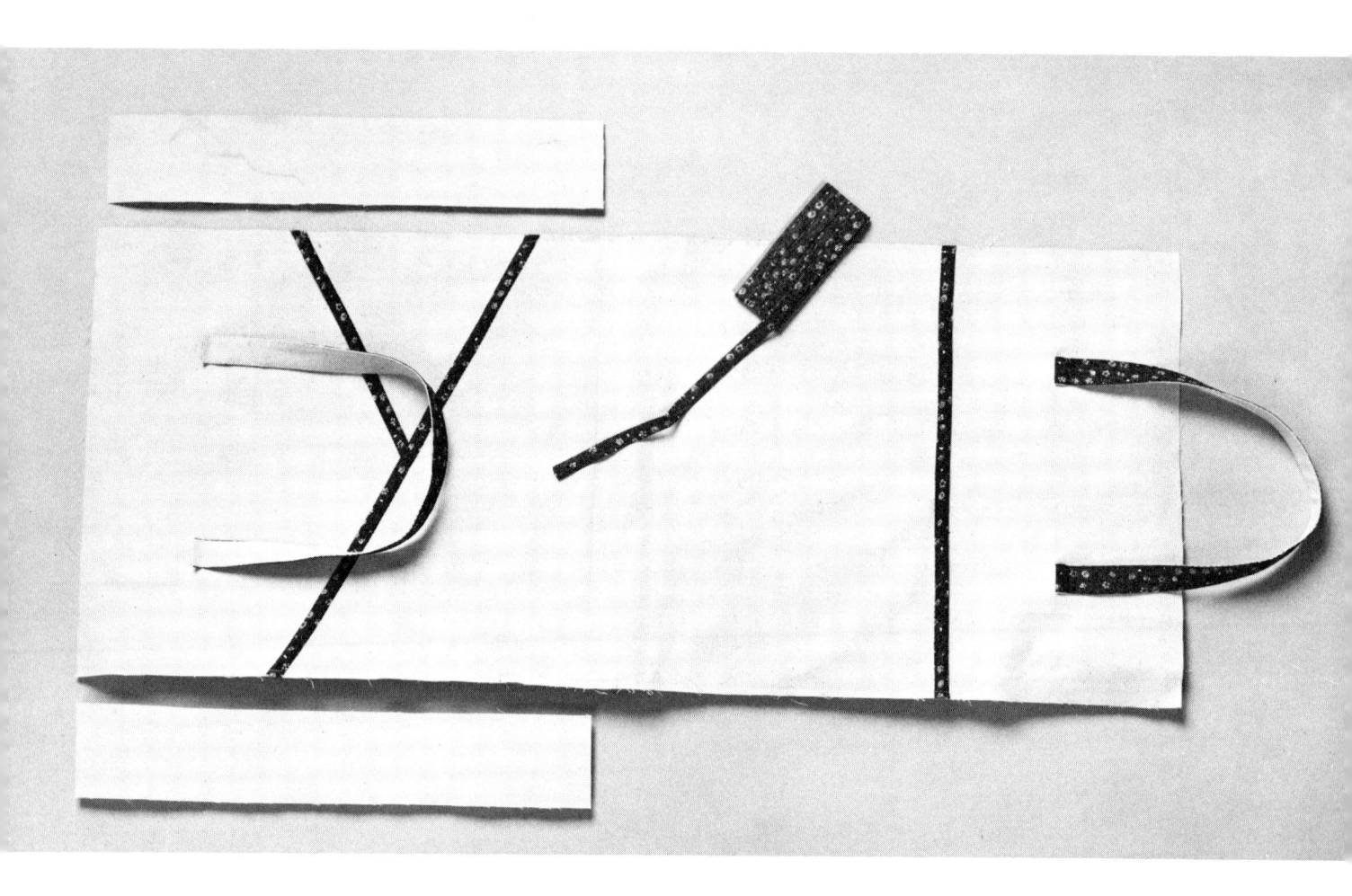

a. Use light- to medium-weight canvas or denim. Cut a rectangle 37 inches x 15 inches, two side panels 17½ inches x 3 inches, and two handles 21 inches x 2½ inches along the selvage. Cut one pocket 15 inches x 12½ inches at one end, slanted to 4½ inches at the other end, and one pocket 15 inches x 23 inches at one end, slanted to 15 inches at the other. You will need one pack of wide (1-inch) printed bias binding and one of regular-width matching printed bias binding for trim, or you may use the wide width entirely, two packs in all.

Bind the slanted edges of both pockets and the straight edge of the longer one with the wide binding. Center the pockets on the bag rectangle, as shown, the short one first and the long one covering it. Run two rows of machine stitching across the pockets, 3 inches apart along the base of the bag (the rows of stitching should be 17 inches from each end of the bag rectangle). Run machine stitching along the sides, less than ¼ inch from the raw edges, to hold the pockets in place.

Make up the handles as described for those cut on the selvage in Chapter 1, and stitch the wide bias on the outside as a decoration. Sew the handles in place about 4 inches below the top of the bag and about 7 inches apart.

b. When the seams of a side-panel bag are sewed on the outside and finished with bias binding, you will have to hem the top of each piece before seaming. Start by matching and pinning the side panel in place from the center bottom (page 36), clip the outer piece just deeply enough to enable it to turn around the corner and make sure that the top ends come out the same length, before hemming.

If you trim with the regular width bias, as we did, you will stitch a seam of less than ¼ inch, wrong sides together, before applying the bias. If you trim with the wider bias, make an outside seam of ⅜ inches. The difference in these seam widths will make a small length difference at the top end of the bag. The extra length can be trimmed off. We hemmed the ends 1¼ inches after finishing hem edges with zigzag stitching. The bias binding should be turned under at the top for a clean finish and backstitched for security.

4

The Square Root of All Bags

Almost all countries can trace their bags back to a square of material, brought together at the four corners and tied. Three of these which are still in use are the American bandanna, the Japanese furoshiki, and the Mexican tortilla cloth (pages 50–51). The bandanna is a familiar part of our folk literature, but it differs only in fabric, not in purpose, from the squares of cloth in other parts of the world.

The tortilla cloth is woven on a special loom of just the right width and used to transport that staple of the Mexican diet, a stack of tortillas. The lovely one shown on page 50 was imported by Pan American Phoenix to be sold more as a work of art than as a practical carrier.

The furoshiki can be made of any silk, cotton, or synthetic and is exactly like our square scarves. A new type, sewed along two sides, is now making its appearance in Japanese stores here. We show both kinds on page 51.

We have made an updated version of the bandanna bag, a familiar Mexican woven bag, and the newer seamed furoshiki. The directions for all three are given here.

1. The bandanna bag is good for beach use. It is made of four bandannas, two red and two blue, and is completely self-lined. Start by measuring and squaring the bandannas—they are usually slightly rectangular. Ours came out to almost 20 inches on each side, after trimming.

Lay one blue bandanna down, right side up. Match the corner and two sides of one red one, right sides together, to two sides of the blue one and pin for seaming. Fold the remaining triangle of the red one back on itself, out of the way. Pin the other red bandanna at the corner and along the other two sides of the blue one in the same way. Stitch these seams, stopping and backstitching 1 inch from each corner, where the red bandannas are folded. Lay the other blue bandanna right side down on the two red ones as they lie folded back, so that the right sides are together. Pin the other seams in the same way as the first and stitch to within 1 inch of the folded corners again, leaving a 4-inch opening in one seam for turning.

At this point you may have to go in blind faith, but start turning the entire many-sided piece through the opening. When it is completely right side out, you can fold it down into itself, as shown, so that it is self-lined. Slipstitch the 4-inch opening closed. Turn the free corners to the wrong side to form the ends of the casing opening. Machine stitch around the folded upper edge to form the casing, run a cord through each separate half of the bag, and knot the ends together.

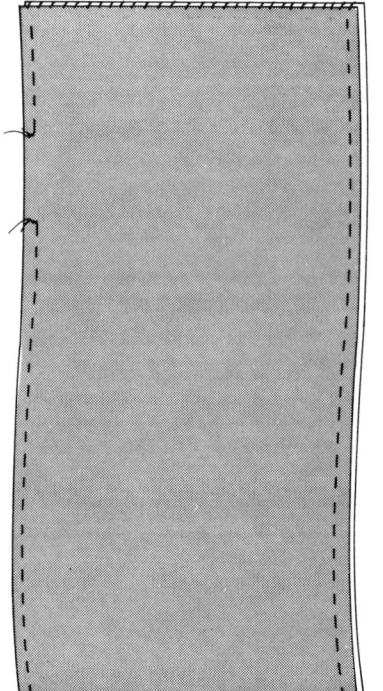

2. The flat Mexican bag is also self-lined. We used ⅜ yard of a lengthwise-striped wool fabric 56 inches wide. After straightening the grain and trimming, we had a piece 13 inches x 56 inches.

Fold the long rectangle right sides together and slipstitch or zigzag the selvage ends together flatly. With the rectangle still folded in this position, seam the raw edges, leaving a 4-inch opening for turning. Turn the bag through this opening and steam the seams open flat by using a sleeve board or a rolled towel. Push the selvage end down inside the other half of the bag, until the selvage is at the fold and the bag is 14 inches long, completely doubled and self-lined. Slipstitch the 4-inch opening closed and tack the seams together so that the lining will stay flatly in place.

Handles can be made of upholstery cord or braided yarn and hand stitched along the seam. We made a short handle with a tassel at each end, but it can be made as long as you like and run all the way down the sides like the ones now made in Mexico.

3. The seamed furoshiki can be made in any size you wish, but the fabric must always be three times longer than it is wide. Ours was cut from ½ yard of 45-inch fabric. We left the selvages on the ends and cut the piece 16 inches wide so that after hemming it was 15 inches x 45 inches. The first step is to hem each raw edge with a narrow shirttail hem.

Lay the rectangle right side down and fold each end up so that it forms a perfect square, three layers thick. Pin the hemmed edge of one end square to the hemmed edge of the center square. Repeat this process

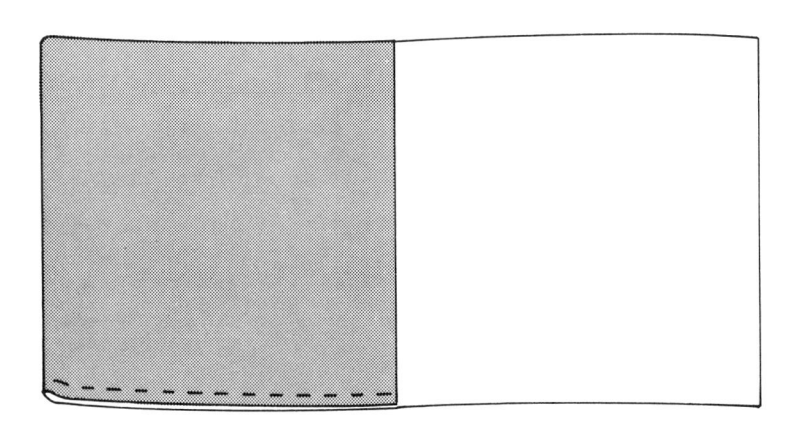

52 THE BIG BAG BOOK

on the opposite side of the other end square. You may then sew the edges together as pinned, stitching by hand or machine as close as possible to the finished edge. You will find that the three layers form a sort of double pocket and that the two free ends can be picked up and tied together quite securely.

There is an extra optional step which helps to prevent ripping at the corners. From the scraps of fabric cut two small squares, not larger than 2 inches on each side. Fold them wrong sides together to form triangles and zigzag the raw edges together; or fold them right sides together, seam them as narrowly as possible, and turn them right side out. Set them into the upper end of each joined edge of the furoshiki like small gussets.

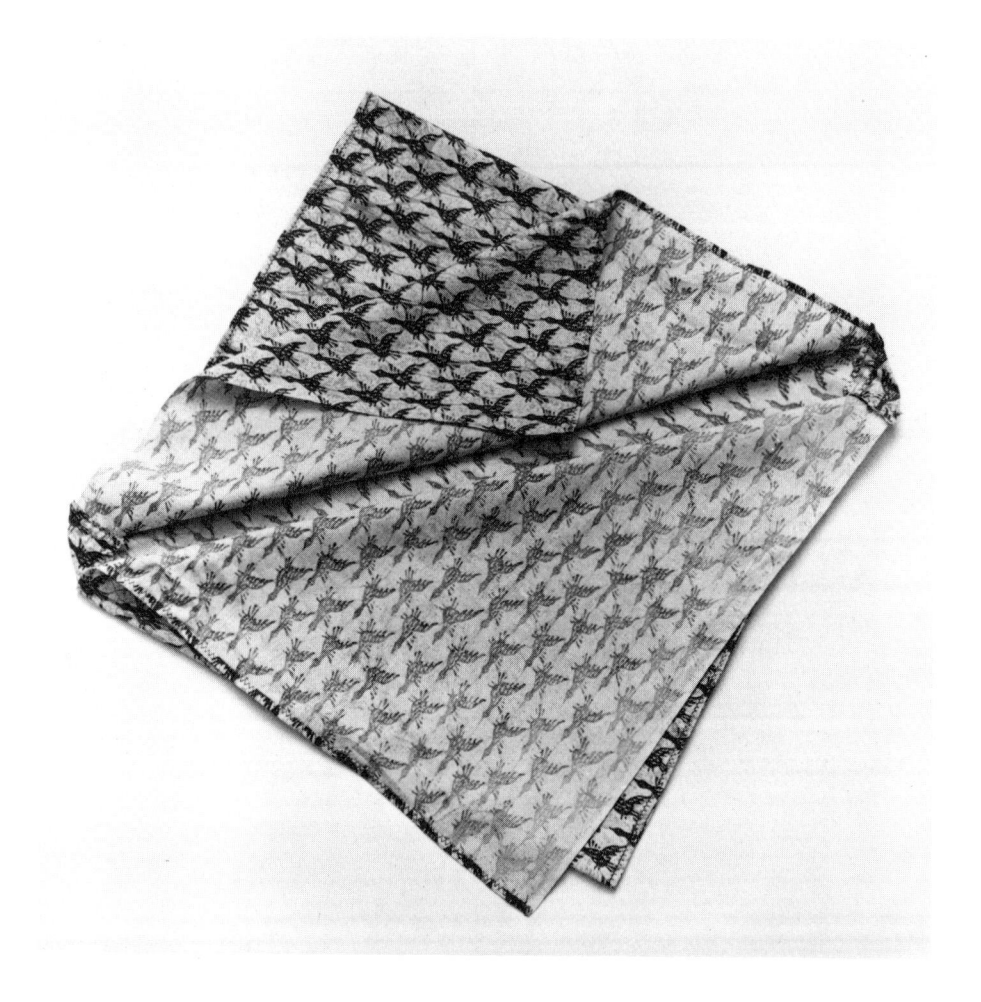

5
Handles Without Care

The best part about the handles available at notions counters is that little care is needed in using them. They're sturdy, inexpensive, and an aid to making super simple bags. They are also made in handsome materials, such as wood and tortoiseshell plastic, which blend with many fabrics. We think they're especially suited to heavy drapery and upholstery fabrics and winter textures like wool, corduroy, and velveteen, plate 4.

Suitable basic shape suggestions usually come with the handles when you buy them. The principles that apply to shaping the other bags can be transferred to bags with handles. Many can be cut like flat bags (page 26), or given more room by adding a side panel or a mitered corner, as in totes (page 35).

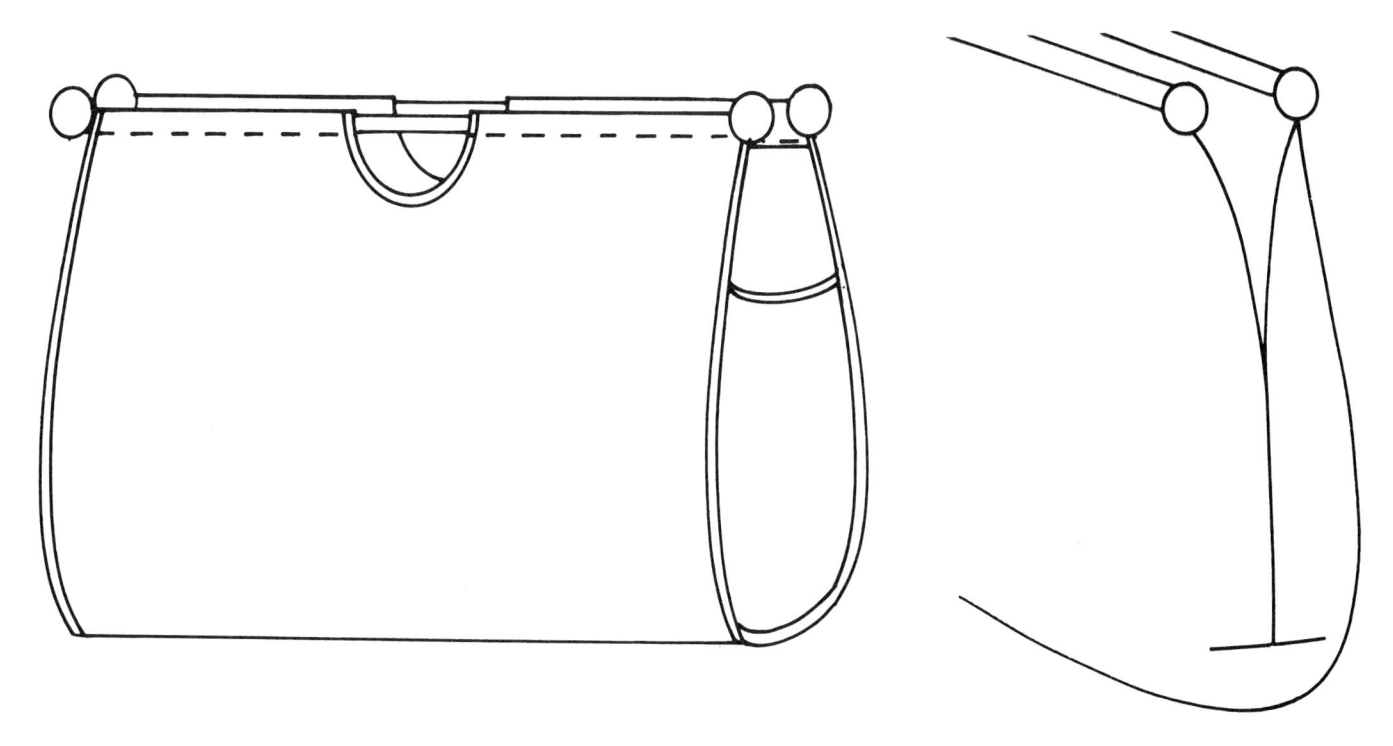

54 THE BIG BAG BOOK

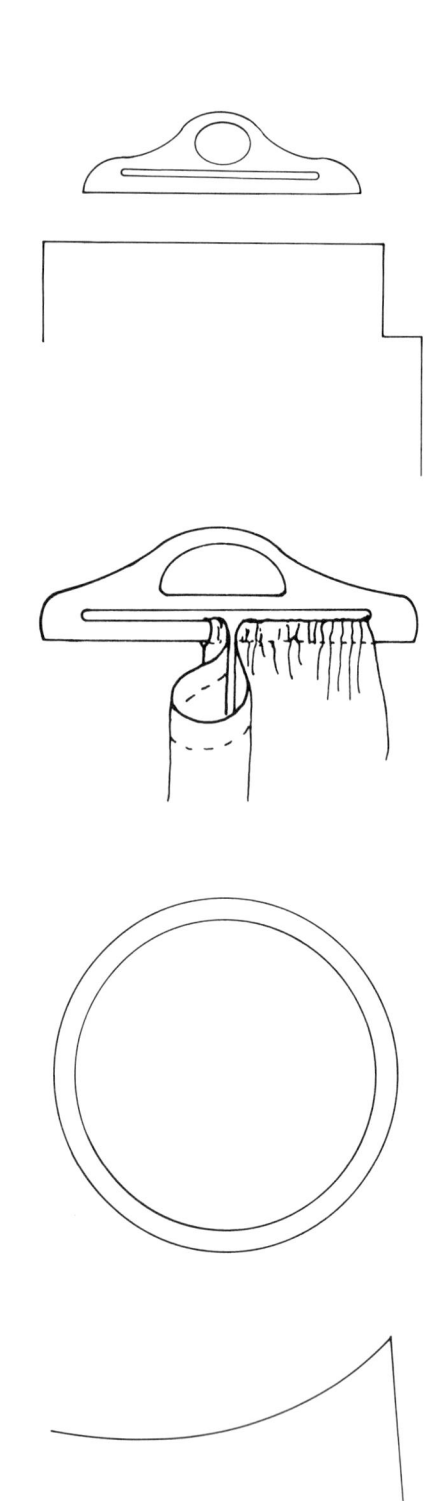

That good old standby of needlewomen, the knitting bag with wooden handles, can be cut full enough to form gathers when mounted on the handles. That means about one and a half the length of the handle slot, plus seams or hems on the sides. The sketch shows another 1½ inches on each side, about 4 inches below the top, to simulate a panel side. It can be mitered to a width of 3 inches at the bottom and finished with a narrow hem or a lining applied by hand at the top. The corners will have to be clipped ½ inch deep before turning the edge for hem or lining.

A newer version of the knitting-bag handle has a narrow opening so that the bag can be hemmed first and then slipped through the opening into the slot.

Ring handles come in several sizes up to the large ones that can be carried way up onto the shoulder so that the bag is tucked securely under the arm. We found that two things helped in designing and constructing bags for any size of ring. Use the Fashion Ruler to draw a long, curved upper edge that will gather back comfortably onto the rings. If you're uncertain of the amount of curve, test your pattern in muslin. We found that an attached casing, cut about 2½ inches wide on the bias, made assembly easier than when we tried to work the curve of the bag itself around the ring.

The rod handles with finials can be used in various ways and are fun because they can be stained, painted, or decorated as your fancy dictates. We even bought longer ⅜-inch dowels to use with one set of finials for our big carpet bag (page 143). The little tortoiseshell ones are ideal for evening bags like our velvet one and should also be a joy to the needlepointer who prefers to finish her own bags.

No type of handle is restricted to one style of bag. Miters, side panels, and offsets can be interchanged for added fullness. We also found that the gusset, borrowed from the furoshiki (page 52), worked well on a ring bag or any other flat bag on handles.

Bags on handles are usually soft, unstiffened, even slightly gathered. In the heavier fabrics you may not want to add a lining. You can simply hem the upper edge to form a casing to slip onto the handles, and narrowly hem the sides below the handles. If a lining is used, set it in by hand along the side opening and at the lower edge of the hem casing (Chapter 1).

We will give you the dimensions and finishes that we used for our group of bags with handles. They should serve only as suggestions to be combined and changed as you find suitable for your material. Almost all of the fabrics used were leftovers, so no yardages are given. If you were to buy fabric, you should start looking on the remnant table, especially in the home-decorating department. In most cases you can make two bags out of no more than ¾ yard of fabric, 45 inches or wider.

1. The dark monogrammed bag is wool flannel, left over from a skirt. We cut two pieces 12 inches deep x 14 inches wide (seams included)

and rounded off the lower corners to a nice shape with the Fashion Ruler. We then measured around the curve on the seamline to within 3 inches of the top—29 inches for a boxing strip. We cut the strip 29 inches x 3 inches (seams included). All lining pieces are identical to the outside, except that the depth of the sides is only 10 inches instead of 12 inches.

After we joined the boxing strips to both the bag and the lining (page 31), we found it quite simple to finish the sides below the casing and the upper edge of the boxing strip with a seam. We pinned the lining right sides together with the bag and stitched a seam along the raw edges, stopping and starting with a backstitch ½ inch below the top edge of the lining. It was easy to turn the whole piece right sides out through the ends, press the lining in place, hem the casing, and turn the lining under against it. That left only the upper edge of the lining to finish by hand against the lower edge of the casing. The monogram is described on page 131.

2. The heavy gold brocade was a bonus from a redecorating project and makes as good a knitting bag as it did dining chairs. We call it the "one-hour bag" and think it makes a dandy gift for needleworking friends. Ours is cut in one piece, 15 inches wide and 30 inches long. We constructed it like the basic tote (page 35), with a 3-inch miter at each lower corner. Because it was to go on handles, we also left a 4-inch opening down from the top of each side seam. Because the fabric is very heavy, we finished all the hem edges with zigzag stitching. The casing is 1 inch deep and stitched by machine. Not more than one hour from beginning to end!

3. The print bag on the 11-inch rod is also a home-decorating bonus, a fine, firm cotton drapery fabric with stain-resistant finish. We were able to cut this in one long strip, 15 inches x 22 inches, with an offset of 4 inches x 1½ inches taken out of the ends of each side. The strap handles were cut 3 inches x 16 inches each and finished to 1 inch wide. The miter is 2½ inches. There is no lining and everything is machine finished. The strap handles are incorporated with the top hem casing, as it is stitched.

4. There are other ways of treating the rod and finial, including the slightly gathered velvet evening purse (page 112). One of our favorites is the hole-for-a-handle trick which we made in heavy brown canvas with calico bias binding trim. The main piece was cut 10 inches x 23 inches, and the side panels 7½ inches x 2 inches, using the selvage for the upper end to reduce bulk. The hole is cut 5 inches deep and 4½ inches wide, the curve shaped with a compass. A compass was also used to shape the lower end of the side panel. The zipper pocket is 8 inches x 5½ inches finished, with a 7-inch zipper (Chapter 1). There are no seam allowances except those along the zipper edges of the pocket pieces, because everything is joined and finished with regular-width bias binding. You will need one pack for a bag this size.

5. The soft velveteen bag on 8-inch rings started as two 9-inch x 13-inch rectangles, leftovers, of course. We rounded off all the edges and made the top curve with the Fashion Ruler, being careful to plan for the nap running up on both pieces. The casing is a 13-inch-x-3-inch bias piece of the fabric. We added two little gussets, 2 inches square (page 52), to keep from ripping the seams with use.

After seaming the lower curve and inserting the gussets, we decided that it might be possible to install the casing by machine. We started by turning under the raw edges at the sides of the bag and the raw ends of the casing strip and pinning them right sides together. The long edge of the casing was easy to curve along the upper edge of the bag and stitch by machine, taking slightly less than ½-inch seam. Then came the hard part! We folded the casing over the ring so that the two long raw edges of the casing met. We used the zipper foot to stitch through both layers of the casing and into the bag along the same seamline we'd used before. We found it helpful to tack the ends together firmly by hand before starting. Stitching in such an awkward place requires some care and patience, moving the casing along the ring to keep a flat area just ahead of the machine foot. If you hate such gymnastics, make the last seam by hand with a backstitch. We finished the bag with a silk-print lining, cut just like the two sides of the bag and installed by hand (Chapter 1).

The handles used here are all made by David Traum and sold inexpensively at notions counters.

PLATE 1. Totes, in a variety of sizes, shapes, and textures, provide a fashionable answer to the ubiquitous paper shopping bag. Chapter 3.

PLATE 2. Ultrasuede makes clutch purses that could easily pass for the best suede. Chapter 12.

PLATE 3. Two convertible shoulder bags from the same pattern, each with its own fashion look. Chapter 12.

PLATE 4. Handles help in making very professional-looking bags with scraps of interesting fabrics. Chapter 5.

PLATE 5. Reverse appliqué produces startling color effects and can be designed as you go. Chapter 14.

PLATE 6. The classic designs from American quilts make up-to-date decorations for bags. Chapter 14.

PLATE 7. Hanger bags, fold-up bags, and all manner of soft travel bags can be carried on and packed away. Chapter 9.

PLATE 8. Books, beads, and money can all be gift wrapped in their own bags. Chapter 16.

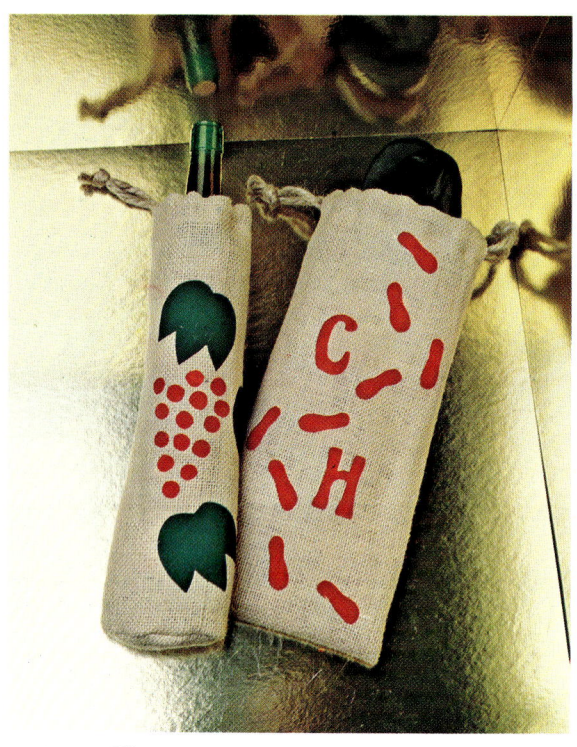

PLATE 9. Slippers or a bottle of wine are equally at home wrapped in burlap. Chapter 16.

PLATE 10. Turnabout nonsense bags for rain and shine or political mugwumps. Chapter 16.

PLATE 11. Christmas and birthday totes can be given with the gifts. Chapter 16.

PLATE 12. Toys tucked away in their own carriers are never out of place, a joy for owners and mothers. Chapter 10.

PLATE 13. Picnicking in the park or at the beach can be all the better with fold-up and roll-up bags. Chapter 8.

PLATE 14. Evening bags can be practical as well as pretty, as proved by the tote and furoshiki. Chapter 13.

PLATE 15. Glitter and glamour make a gala evening and a perfect tiny bag to carry along. Chapter 13.

6
Sport Your Own Bag

Games and sports require an enormous amount of equipment, and equipment requires handy carriers. With a little thought and planning it is possible to corral the necessary balls, rackets, shirts, and shorts into one bag. It is possible to provide space for a wet bathing suit or to take game boards to the beach with the checkers and chess folded neatly inside.

In many cases you will want to measure your own piece of equipment and plan your own bag, just as we have done for the large tent. Be sure that your measurements are accurate—it never hurts to measure twice and write it down each time. Plan for all the pockets when you're estimating yardage. Be sure that zippers are available in the sizes you need or that you can cut them to a shorter length or use two, face to face, when you need very long ones. Make paper or muslin patterns and double-check to see that everything fits and you've remembered to allow seams. As with all the bags we've shown before, it is easier to sew on pockets, handles, and so on, before joining the pieces of the bag together.

1. The problems of storing and carrying a large four-man tent can be solved with a nicely fitted bag, based on the duffle bag, Chapter 2. Zippers and pockets are described in Chapter 1.

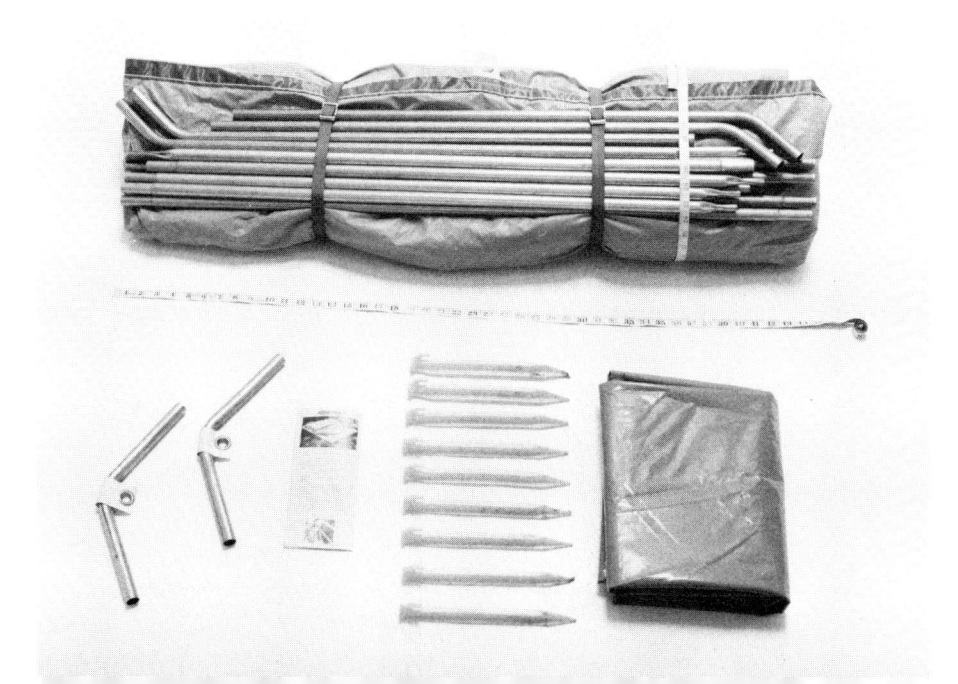

a. Fold the tent and arrange it compactly with the long sections of the poles as a guide for total length. Measure length and circumference, allowing a little extra room for the ground cloth and short pole pieces to go in the main section of the bag. Measure the stakes and plan a pleated pocket to allow them enough room. Plan a flat pocket for keeping the directions handily on the outside.

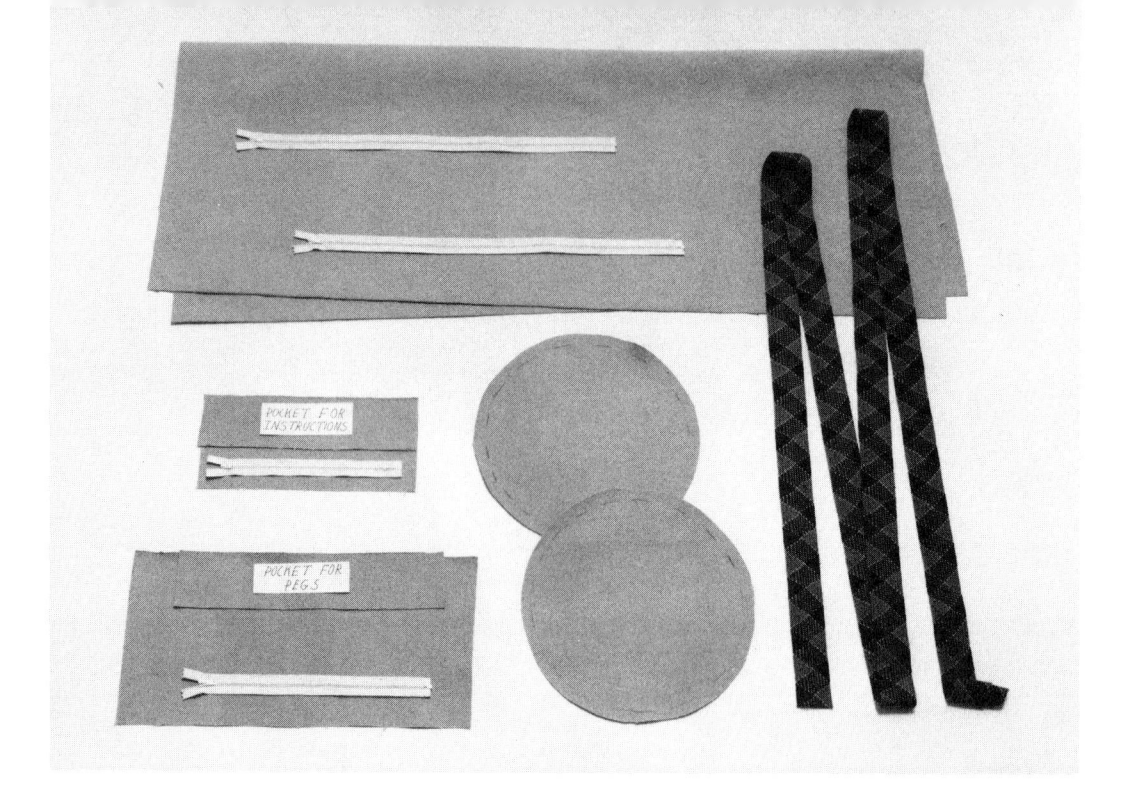

b. This large tote required 2 yards of 36-inch-wide heavy cotton canvas, two 22-inch zippers to make up the total length of the bag, one 10-inch zipper for the flat pocket, and one 12-inch separating zipper for the pleated pocket. The handles took 3½ yards of 2-inch-wide cotton webbing. In cutting, remember to use selvages whereever possible to reduce bulk. Finish all other raw edges with stitching, preferably zigzag.

c. Sew the pockets on each side, several inches below the long edges that form the zipper opening. Make a wraparound handle (page 31) and sew it outside of the pockets to a point a few inches from the zipper edge. In this case the handles are long enough to allow the bag to be carried from the shoulder.

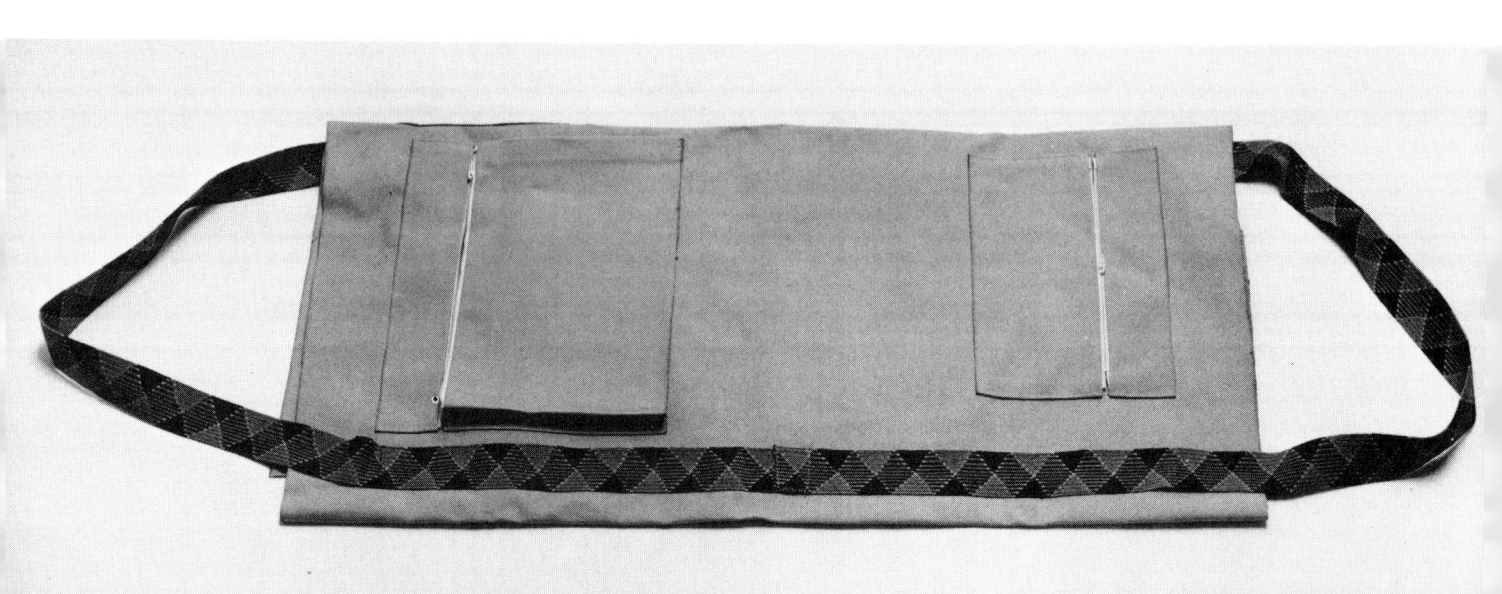

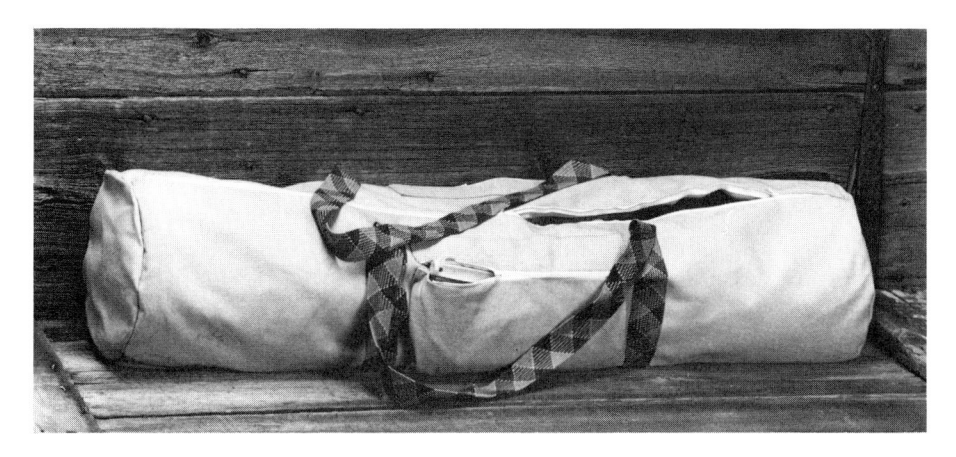

d. The bag is completed by sewing the two zippers in place, both opening from the center outward, and then seaming the circular ends to the ends of the tubular piece, remembering to leave zippers open so that the bag can be turned right side out. Any points of strain can be restitched for reinforcement.

2. A tennis bag should be nice enough, large enough, and complete enough to go straight from home to the office to the tennis club. Our large tennis tote includes a zipper pocket on the outside for money and cards so that you can leave your purse at home and a zipper closing for the top so that shorts, balls, sweaters, and even shoes can be tucked away out of sight.

You will need 1¼ yards of heavy canvas. We made the zipper inset

60 THE BIG BAG BOOK

from a scrap of a contrasting color to match the binding. One package of wide (1-inch) bias binding trimmed the outside pockets. The separating top zipper is 14 inches and the pocket one is 12 inches.

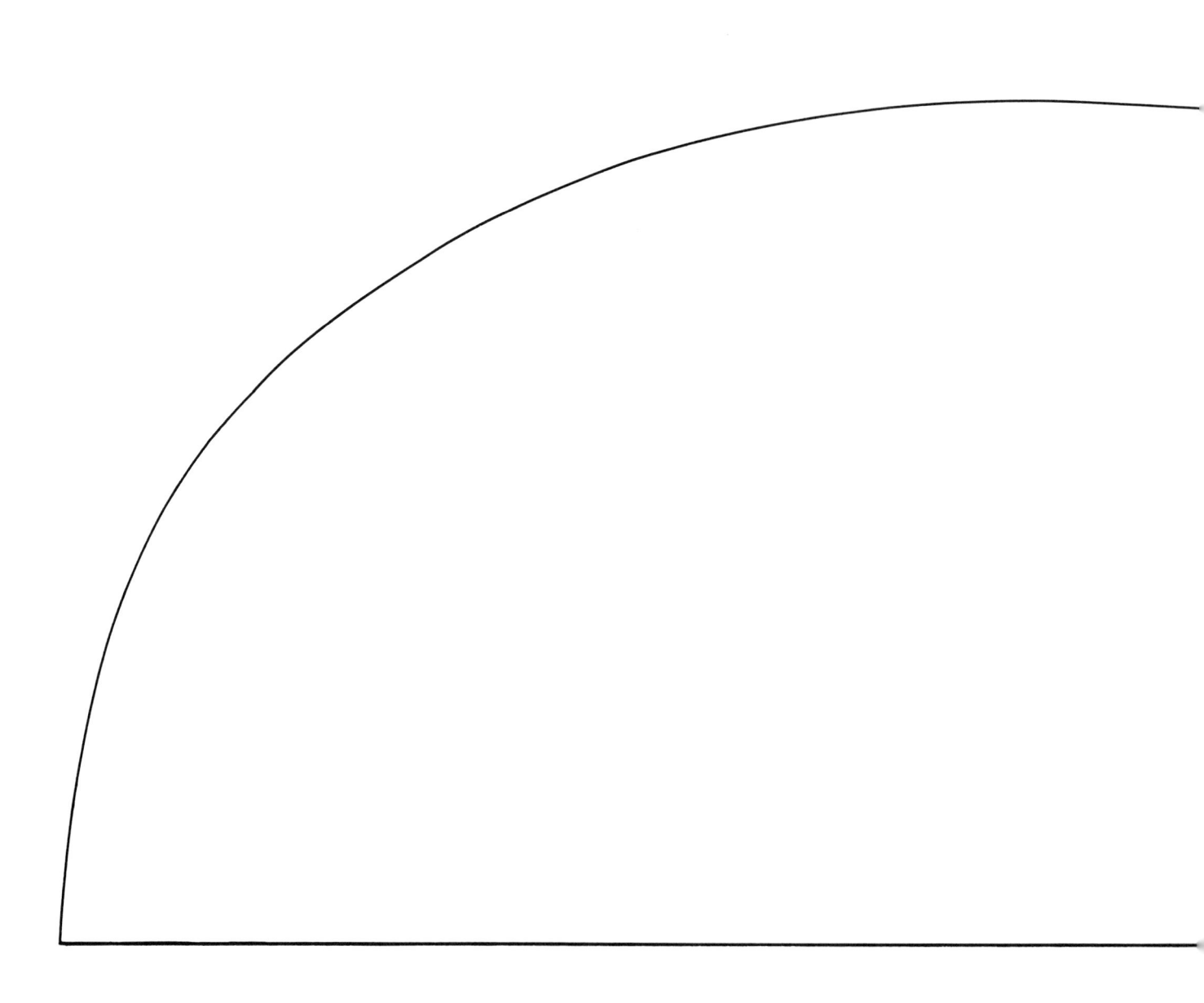

Refer to the big tote bag on page 39 for constructing the zipper inset. Cut bag rectangle 22 inches x 36 inches, pocket pieces (Chapter 1) 12 inches x 8 inches and 12 inches x 2 inches, the zipper inset pieces 15½ inches x 3 inches, and the racket pocket by the pattern. Insert zippers in both pockets and bind around the edges. Stitch them in place. The racket pocket opens enough to slip the racket in even without the ends being left unstitched as we did and tied in place, but we found this finish a little handier. Place the handles near the top and out of the way of the pockets, as shown. You can make them long enough to carry on the shoulder or shorter, as you prefer. As with any tote the last step is to sew the sides and miter the bottom corners, 3½ inches in this case.

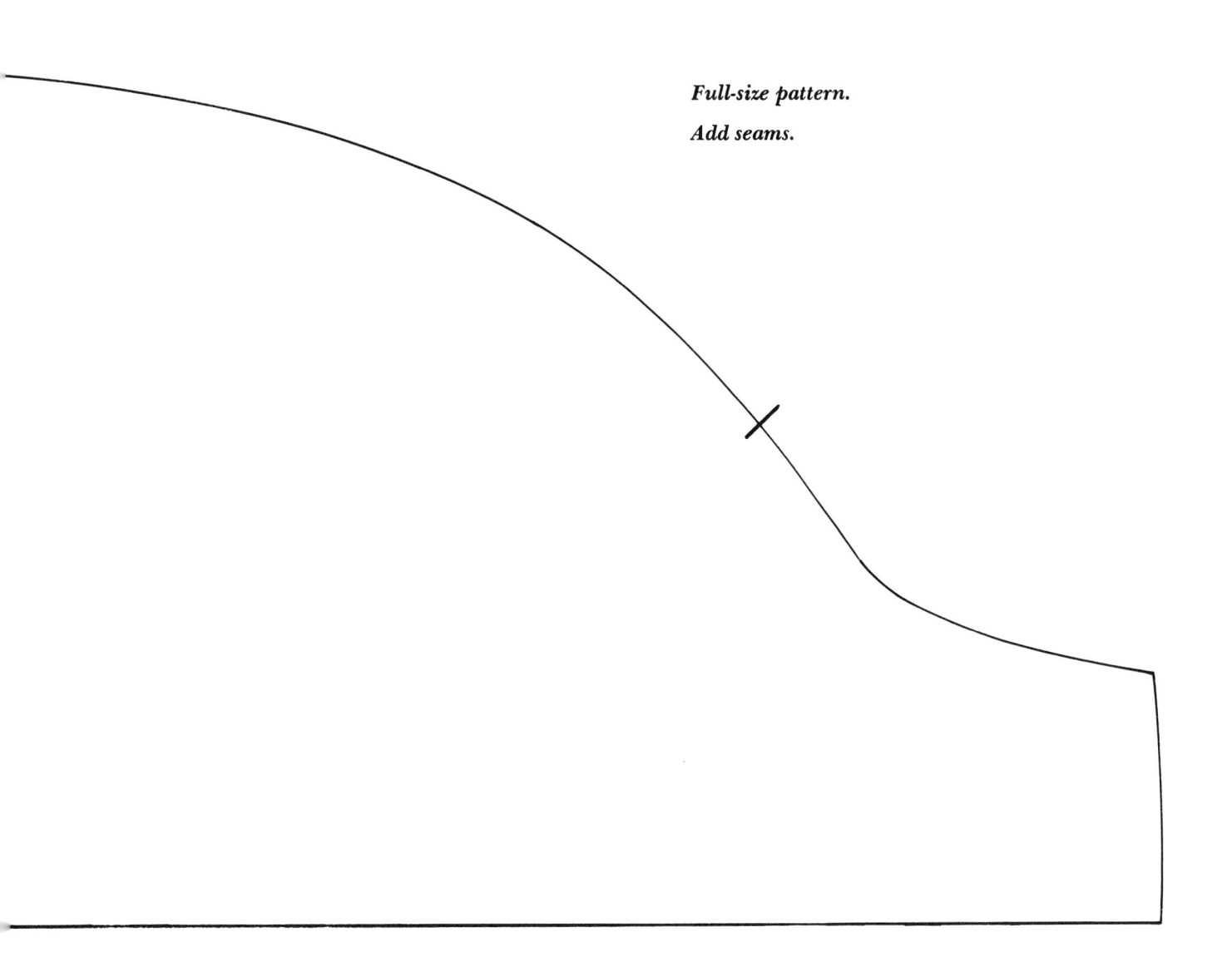

Full-size pattern.

Add seams.

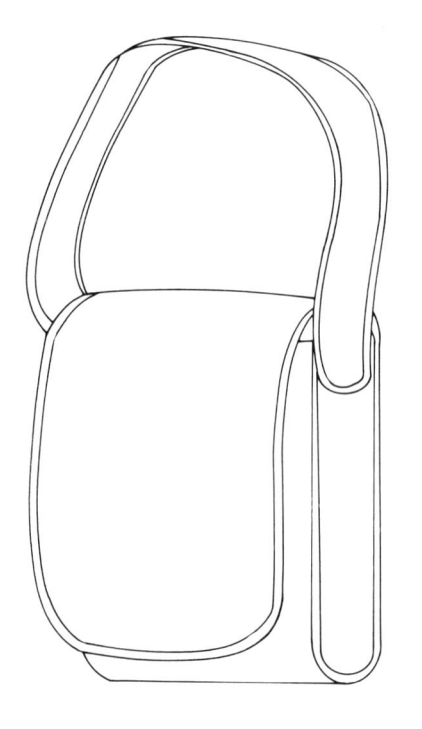

3. The swim and gym bag, like the tennis tote, can carry you through the day, with a trip to the health club included. It even has a waterproof pocket for that wet bathing suit. The green bag on the cover and the child's book bag (Chapter 14) are made by the same versatile pattern. You need 1⅛ yards of heavy canvas, 36 inches wide, and two packages of wide (1-inch) bias binding or 6 yards of binding cut from your own fabric (the cut width should be 2 inches to allow the edges to turn under). We used an 8-inch zipper for the waterproof pocket and an inexpensive 2-inch slide buckle and grippers to make the strap length adjustable.

Cut the main bag piece 38 inches x 13 inches and round off the corners at one end for the flap. Cut the side panels 12 inches x 3½ inches, using the selvage for the top end to avoid bulk and rounding off the bottom end for easier sewing and binding. Cut a front pocket, 7 inches x 10 inches, to go under the flap and a back pocket 12½ inches x 20 inches. Cut a lining 12½ inches x 20 inches of medium-weight pliable plastic, available in houseware departments. If you wish to make the straps adjustable as we did on this bag and the one on the cover, cut two pieces, each 2 inches wide, one 10 inches long, and one 30 inches long. Round both ends of the longer piece and one end of the shorter one. If you don't want an adjustable strap, cut one 2-inch-wide piece to the desired length.

Baste the waterproof lining to the wrong side of the larger pocket. Sew the zipper to the two ends and seam the sides together, leaving the zipper open for turning. Miter the lower corners about 1 inch and turn the pocket right side out. Place the pocket with the zipper end roughly 13 inches from the flap end of the main bag piece. (You should check to see exactly what area will be the back of the bag after sewing it to the side panels.) By opening the zipper you will be able to get the machine foot inside the pocket to sew two rows of stitching across to secure the pocket to the bag—it will hang free at the bottom. Place the rows just below the zipper, about $\frac{1}{4}$ inch apart, and backstitch at each end.

Bind around the other pocket and sew it to the front of the bag, with the opening 2 inches below the bag edge. The side panels are sewed in as described on page 36, taking only a $\frac{1}{4}$-inch seam with the wrong sides together. We found that if we started the selvage end of the side panel $\frac{3}{8}$ inch below the front edge of the bag, we could then bind that front edge, down around the side panel and continuously around the flap and the other side panel. The straps are bound and stitched securely to the top of the side panels. Sew the buckle on the end of the short piece and arrange the grippers, using four top gripper pieces and two bottom ones, so that the strap can be adjusted through the buckle.

64 THE BIG BAG BOOK

4. If you like to take your volley ball to the local gym or down to the beach in the hope of working up a game, you'll find it easier to suspend it from your wrist. The ball pattern given here will fit a standard volley ball, which is a little over 26 inches around.

If you want to make a pattern for any other kind of ball, measure around it, add an inch or two, and mark out two cross lines on a piece of paper to get the dimensions of the pattern piece. The long line should be almost, but not quite, half the circumference. The short cross line, placed at the center of the long one, should be one-eighth of the circumference. Use the curved Fashion Ruler to round out the curved shapes, touching each end of each cross line (see our pattern shape).

Full-size pattern.
Add seams.

FOLD

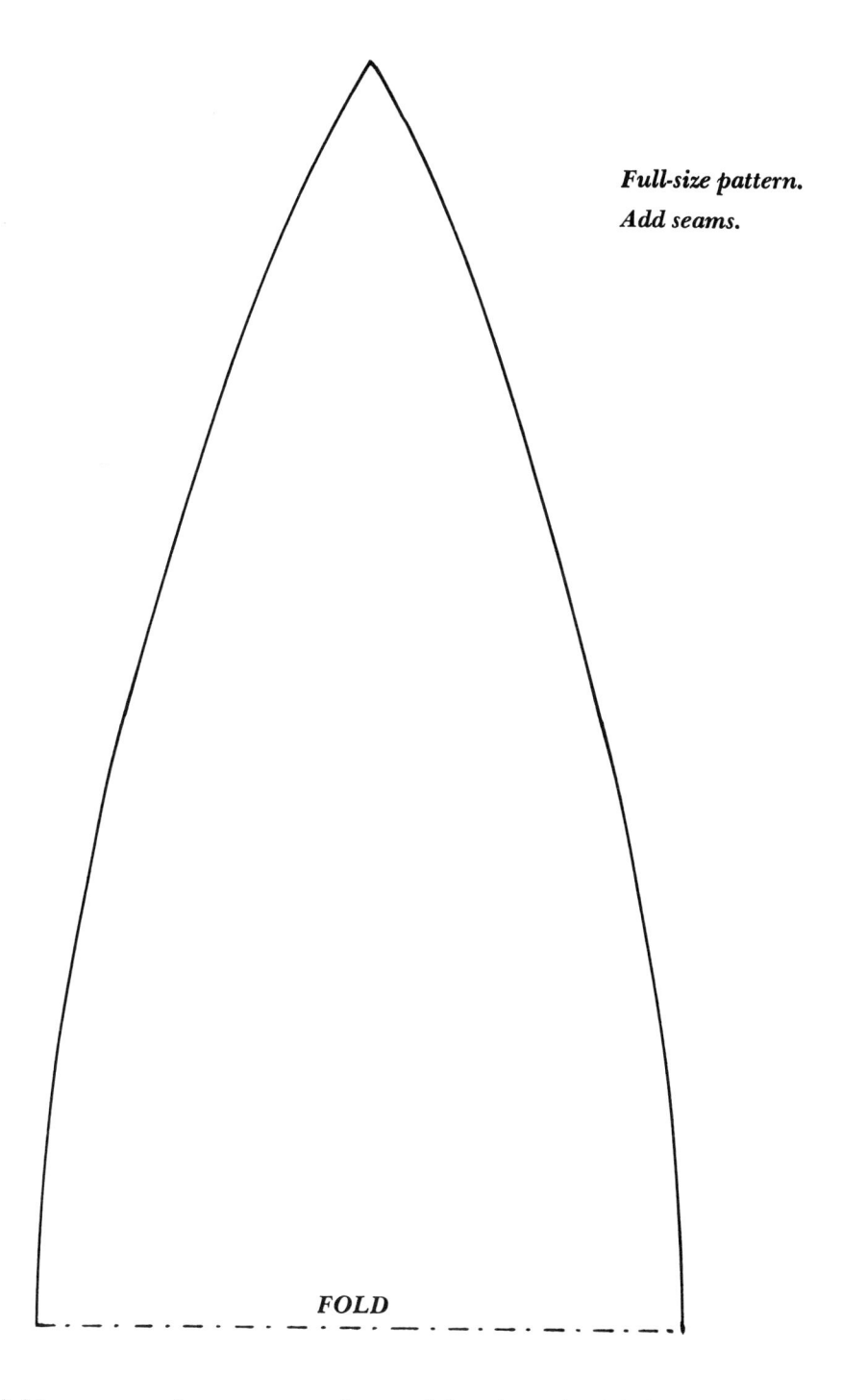

Add seams to the pattern and cut eight pieces in fabric the weight of denim. Seam two groups of four pieces each together to form half balls. If you stitch only to the point of the seamline and not all the way to the raw edge, then backstitch, the ends will be neater. We finished the seams by zigzagging them $\frac{1}{4}$ inch from the stitching line and trimming the excess.

Make a wrist strap about 8 inches long, fold it, and insert it in the last seam. Stitch a zipper about 4 inches longer than the segments in this seam also. Our segments are 14 inches along the curved edges, our zipper is 18 inches.

5. In mid-July on the beach even volley ball may seem like just too much exertion. In that case you'll be glad to have your game-board bag along. Checkers, chess, or backgammon will be sure to interest someone —even four can play on the two boards.

Cut the outer piece 17 inches x 35 inches of a firm denim or canvas. Cut two pieces of Pellon® Fleece 17 inches x 17½ inches, and two pieces of lightweight cotton the same size (one of ours is white, one bright blue). You will also need one package of wide (1-inch) bias binding, 3 yards of webbing for the handles, and two 16-inch separating zippers. We used red for the squares on the blue background and both red and blue for the backgammon triangles on the white.

Make the two patterns in cardboard so that you can draw around them as for quilt pieces. On the right side of the fabric, trace around the patterns to make 32 red squares, 12 blue triangles, and 12 red triangles. Cut ¼ inch beyond the lines, place all the pieces to form 16-inch boards,

Full-size patterns.
Add seams.

leaving 1 inch plain on one edge of each and ½ inch on the other three edges. Alternate the colors of the backgammon triangles, starting with red on the left on each side. Proceed with care, measuring and pinning to keep the boards as accurate as possible. Use the zigzag stitch, set at medium width and fine length, to appliqué each piece in place. With fine, sharp scissors trim close to the stitching before stitching the next piece. On the checkerboard stitch all four sides of the squares at the edge with the 1-inch border. Let the other squares run off into the ½-inch borders; they will be covered with the bias binding. The same treatment is given to the wide ends of the backgammon triangles.

When both boards are finished and pressed, pin them to the Pellon® and machine quilt around each shape. Sew wraparound handles to the outside of the denim. Seam the two boards together on the ends with the 1-inch border, taking up ½ inch and leaving a space of 1 inch between the actual boards. Press that seam open flat and stitch it wrong side down to the wrong side of the denim, across the center where it will fold, baste and bind around the edges. Stitch the zippers along the binding on each side so that they will close tightly down at the fold when zipped, leaving no space for checkers to fall out.

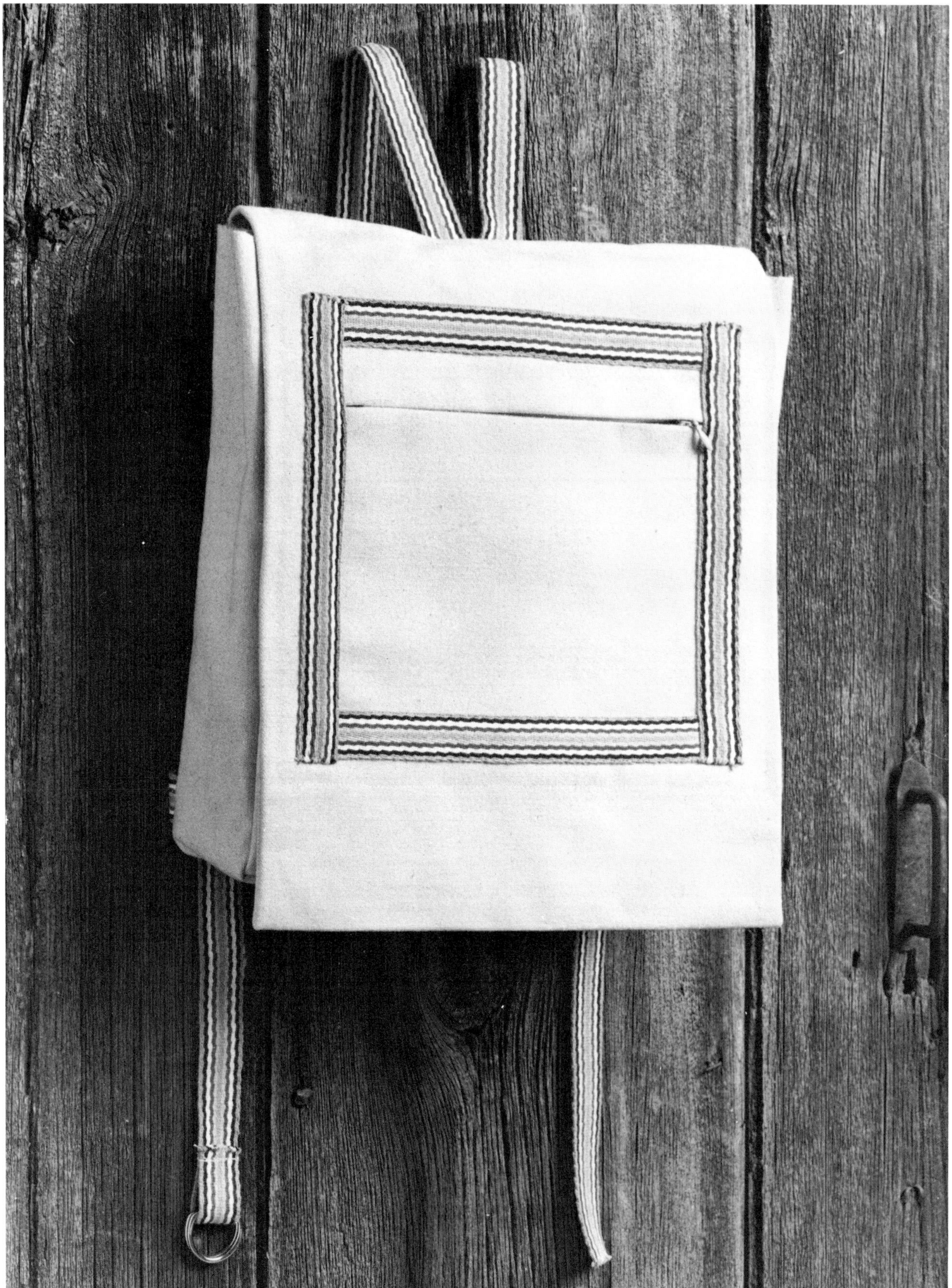

7
Packing It In

There was a time when backpacks were something that most of us had heard about but very few of us had seen, let alone used. All of a sudden our urban society took to the hills and the roads and the air, carrying as much as possible on the back.

In the general trend to mobility came a renewed interest in bicycles. Bike touring means carrying equipment for several days, but even bike use for grocery shopping demands storage space. Panniers for the back fender are a perfect answer. Freedom is what packs are all about, so the belt purse is again in style, and also perfect for bicyclists—or anyone who needs free hands.

We've made versions of these various packs based on the boxed bags and panel-sided bags (Chapter 2). The fabrics must be firm and sturdy, so we've chosen heavy canvas and rip-stop nylon. The canvas makes a handsomer bag but the rip-stop is lightweight and packs into minimum space when not in use. It is available in camp-supply stores, either coated for rain protection or uncoated.

1. Our day pack is large enough to carry all of a hiker's needs, such as lunch and extra jackets, or to be used as a school bag. It will fit a small-to-medium-size teenager or adult. A little simple arithmetic will make it possible to change the size.

You will find one version of this bag shown in this chapter in canvas and the same bag, in a lighter chino, decorated with patchwork in Chapter 14. The main difference is that the straps on the chino bag are made of the fabric, folded and stitched (Chapter 1), and the ones on the canvas are of heavy cotton webbing. Use 1 yard of 36-inch or wider canvas and 4 yards of webbing for the heavier bag, and 1¼ yards of chino, 45 inches or wider, for the other.

For both bags cut a back-and-flap piece 14 inches x 33 inches and a front piece 14 inches x 15 inches. For the lighter bag cut a boxing strip 4½ inches x 41 inches; for the canvas bag cut two boxing strip pieces 4½ inches x 20 inches with a selvage at one end, to be seamed together at the other end.

The diagram shows where to place all straps, D-rings, and Velcro®.

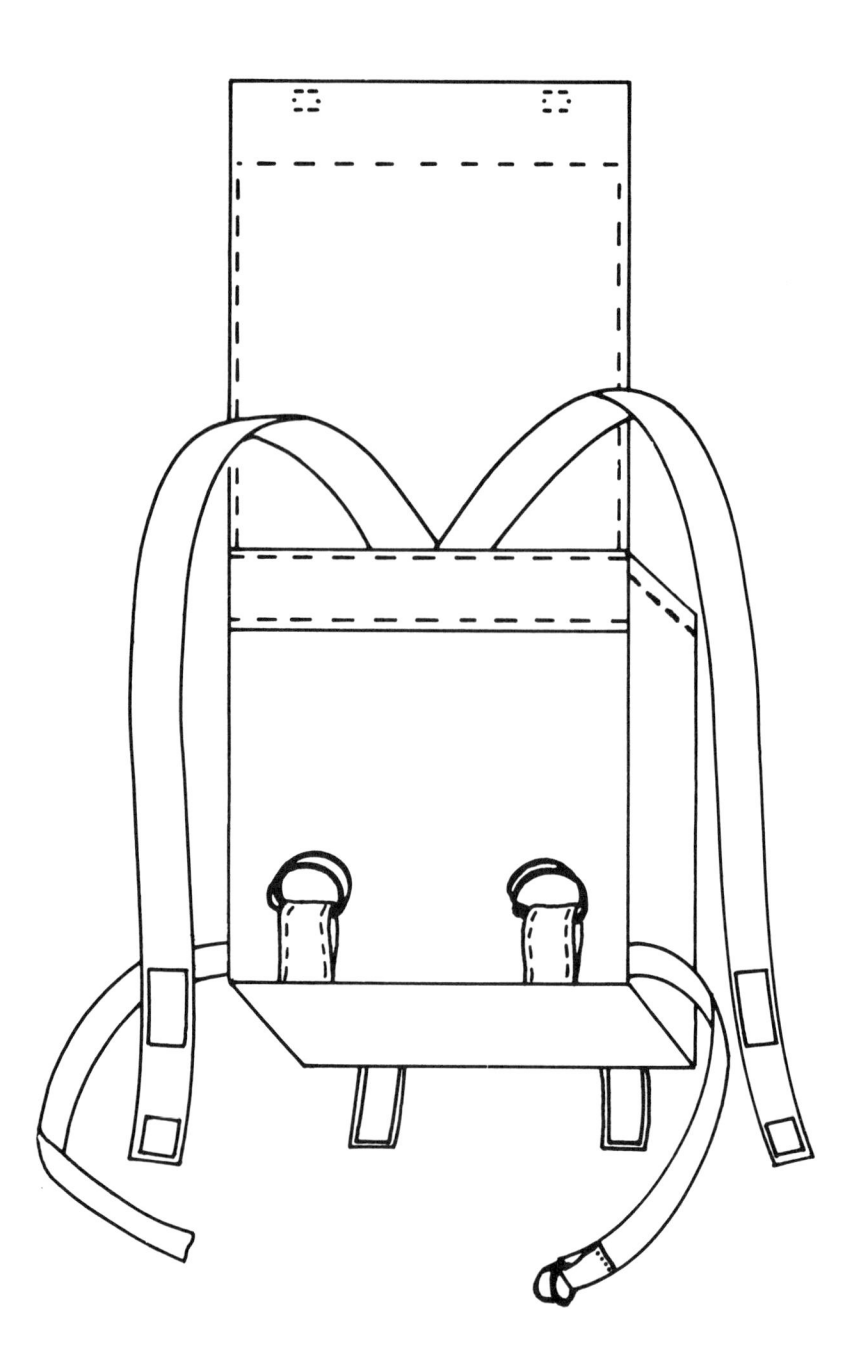

You will need three sets of D-rings and 8 inches of Velcro®. Study the diagram carefully and work in the following order:

a. For lightweight bag make straps of fabric so that they are 1 inch wide finished, and cut a back brace, 3½ inches x 14 inches, to anchor the ends of the shoulder straps. For both bags cut shoulder straps in two parts, 6 inches and 18 inches, to allow slight length adjustment. Cut the waist strap in two pieces, about 20 inches each. Cut two front tabs, 4 inches, to allow adjustment of flap for added carrying capacity. Use the remainder of the webbing for back brace and to trim a zipper flap pocket on the canvas bag.

b. Cut Velcro® into two 3-inch pieces and two 1-inch pieces. Mix and match so that long pieces go with short ones, allowing adjustment in length. Sew pieces to straps as shown in diagram, keeping two short pieces for flap after hemming.

c. Hem top of front piece 1 inch. On lightweight fabric hem ends of boxing strip 1 inch; on canvas seam two pieces of boxing strip together. Attach shoulder straps to back piece with back brace. The top edge of brace should be 13½ inches from the lower edge of back piece.

d. Stitch boxing strip in place, incorporating all straps in seams, as shown in diagram.

e. Hem flap, ½ inch along sides and 3 inches at end. Attach D-rings to straps and sew last piece of Velcro® under flap to match front tabs.

f. Make a zipper pocket, as described in Chapter 1, for the canvas bag and attach it to the flap by sewing strips of webbing along the sides and ends so that it will be decorative as well as useful.

2. The bike panniers are based on the panel-sided bag, with an extension strap added, very much like the swim and gym bag on page 62. The trick is to make them fit the carrier frame and not interfere with heels or wheels. We made the ones shown here to fit a standard 3-speed bike. Each bag is 10 inches on each side and 2½ inches deep when finished.

72 THE BIG BAG BOOK

You will need 1 yard of 36-inch or wider canvas and 5 yards of strong cotton webbing. Five slide buckles, preferably the type with teeth to grip the webbing, will secure everything.

Cut two main pieces, 11 inches x 36 inches, and four side panels, 10½ inches x 3½ inches (using the selvage at one end of each). Cut the webbing into four pieces 23 inches long, four pieces 17 inches long, and four pieces 5 inches long.

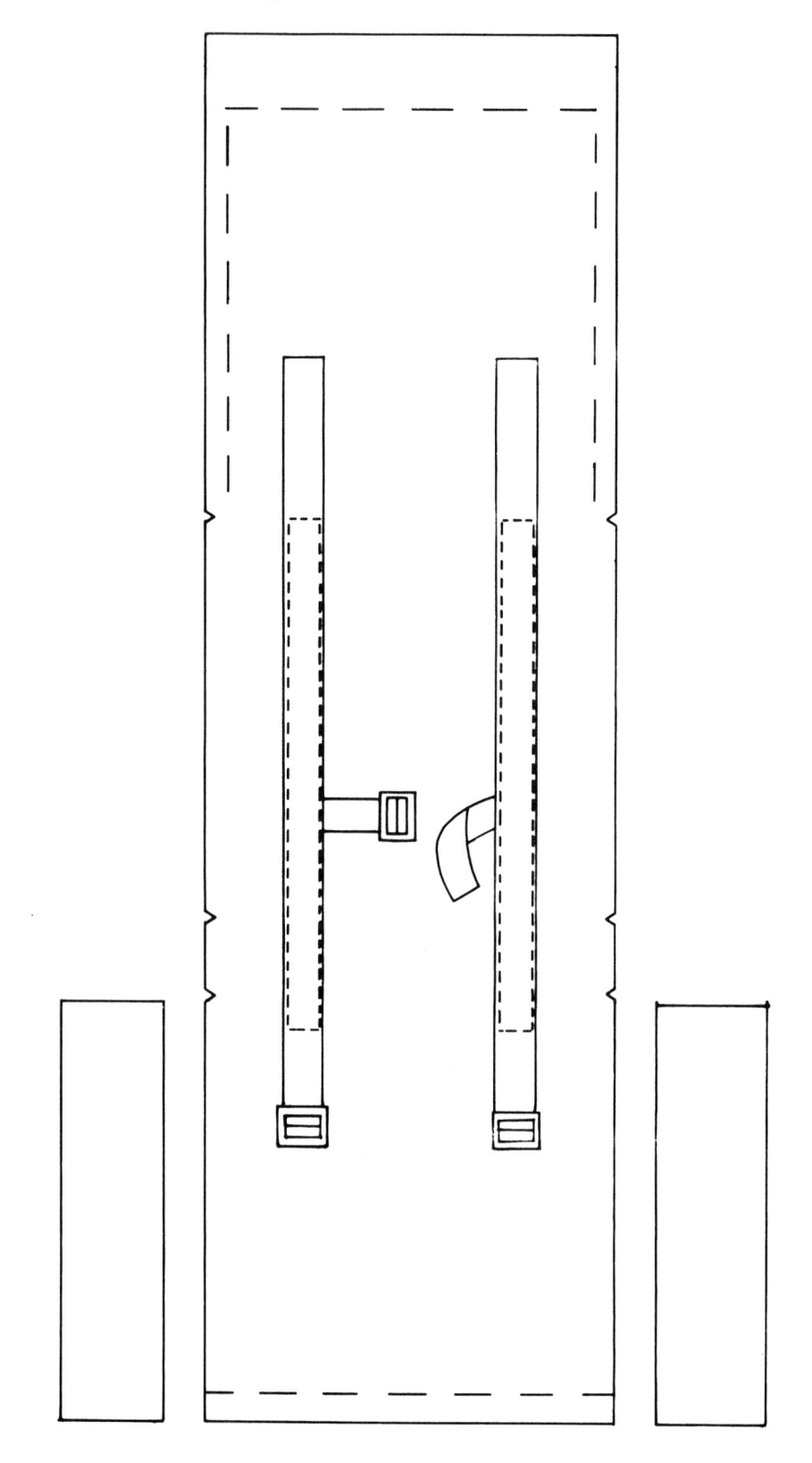

Study the layout carefully and stitch the two long pieces and the two short pieces in place as shown. Leave 5 inches of webbing free at flap end of bag and start stitching 12½ inches from flap end. Stitch for 13½ inches or to a point 10 inches from other end of bag. Hem that end of the main bag piece 1 inch deep. Sew side panels in place. Hem flap ½ inch along sides and 3 inches at end.

Stitch the other strap pieces to the flap, bringing the stitching close up under the 5-inch free piece of the long straps, and leaving a 5-inch free piece on them also. Stitch the 5-inch free pieces of the long straps on one bag to those on the other, laying them double all the way. This double strap should fit across the flat carrier. Sew the other buckles to one pair of the free 5-inch pieces so that they will strap over the carrier clamp for security. The short buckle straps on the backs of the bags are to be fastened around the vertical fender supports.

3. The little belt pack is also made like the swim and gym bag. Cut the main piece 15 inches x 8 inches of heavy canvas or denim. Cut the side panels 5 inches x 1½ inches, using selvage at the top and rounding the bottom. We also rounded off the flap ends to make binding easier.

Before stitching the panels in, you will need to make a carrier on the back to run onto a belt. Cut a piece 5 inches x 3 inches (wider if you use a very wide belt) and bind the short ends. Seam it to the center of the bag piece, one raw edge about 9 inches above the straight end of the piece (this means that the carrier lies up toward the flap end and the seam is 5½ inches from the flap end). Turn it down onto the back, fold under ½ inch, and stitch that edge in place about 7½ inches from the straight end.

Assemble the bag with outside binding like the swim and gym bag, page 62. Use grippers or Velcro® for fastening.

4. The convertible rip-stop nylon pack can be used in many ways. It is especially nice to take along in a large backpack for day trips or in a suitcase when you expect to return with more than you went with. We used ¾ yard of the coated rainproof rip-stop 45 inches wide. It is a simple boxed bag (Chapter 2) with a zipper across the top. It is made convertible by cutting one strap into three parts and adding buckles.

Cut two side rectangles, 18 inches x 14 inches, a boxing strip 42 inches x 7 inches (pieced if necessary), and two zipper strips, 19 inches x 4 inches. Round the corners of the rectangles. Cut webbing 50 inches long for the solid handle and in three pieces, 36 inches, 14 inches, and 14 inches, for the adjustable one.

Sew the long strap piece to one side panel, forming a loop handle at the top. With the 36-inch piece form a loop of the same length on the top of the other side panel. Stitch the straps only about 3 inches below the top, leaving long ends to run through the buckles. Sew the two short pieces at the lower end of that panel, stitching up about 2 inches. Attach prong buckles to the ends of those pieces, using Velcro® to make the length slightly adjustable (backpack, page 71).

Sew the zipper between the zipper strips, attach to one end of the boxing strip, and seam the two side panels in place with the zipper at the handle end (Chapter 2). Adjust the length of the boxing strip on its other end seam if necessary.

8

Fold, Roll, and Picnic in the Park

Picnicking in the park and lying on the beach seem so relaxing if it weren't for packing to get there. We've decided that an all-purpose bag or carrier might make it easier. We also added one little lunch box for the working woman who doesn't want her boss to know that she's brown-bagging in the park from 12:00 to 1:00.

Firm canvas and heavy piqué are the fabrics we chose for durability and a bright, happy look. The shapes are simple and the trimmings and accessories are easily available. You may be able to dream up some personalized variations that suit your special purposes even better. We'll give you dimensions and tips for our versions, plate 13.

1. That little lunch box was made of leftovers of five colors of canvas—it could just as well be denim in only one color. The base is the bottom of a sturdy plastic spring-water bottle, cut off evenly around the edge. We cut it 5½ inches high to make almost a 5½-inch cube, curved a little at the bottom.

Fold, Roll, and Picnic in the Park 77

Start by measuring and making a paper or muslin pattern and trying it on over the plastic. We cut a 6½-inch-x-6½-inch bottom piece and rounded the corners slightly. We cut the side panels 6¾ inches wide (allowing a little ease so the plastic will slip in and out) and 11 inches high. As we seamed the side pieces together, we curved the seams slightly at the bottom end so the sides would fit the bottom piece with only slight easing.

All the seams are finished with zigzag stitching. A casing of 1-inch-wide bias binding is stitched in 2½ inches below the top of the bag. The upper edge is finished with a bias strip of the canvas cut 2 inches wide. For casing and binding see Chapter 1.

2. The handy striped beach bag rolls everything for the whole day into one neat bundle. There's even a pocket in one end that can be stuffed with a towel to serve as a pillow. We bought two very inexpensive white towels. Ours are 42 inches x 24 inches and 24 inches x 16 inches, but you should measure the ones you use and proportion everything accordingly. We used 1⅝ yards of heavy striped cotton, a 22-inch zipper, 2½ yards of 1-inch webbing, and two packs of 1-inch-wide bias binding.

78 THE BIG BAG BOOK

We cut the striped cotton fabric 58 inches x 24 inches so that both towels would fit on it, one lengthwise and one crosswise. We cut a pocket with the stripes running the other way; the finished dimensions are 24 inches x 13 inches. Use the zipper-pocket directions in Chapter 1. Before anything else is stitched, make that pocket and attach it to one end of the long striped piece.

On the same end of the striped piece but on the wrong side, pin the larger towel. Bind one side of the other towel and pin it with the bound edge toward the larger towel.

Make a circle of the webbing, center it, and sew it to the outside (page 31), being sure not to catch the outer pocket or the small towel pocket in the stitching. Bind the edges with bias binding (Chapter 1). We added four ties of double-fold bias to each side in the center section to hold things in the center a little more securely.

3 & 4. Circles are fascinating shapes, and we found they worked well for picnic-in-the-park bags. The red one serves as a tablecloth when open, the yellow one becomes what the children call a "sit-upon."

The yellow bag is ridiculously simple. It requires 1¼ yards of heavy solid-color cotton, 45 inches wide, and the same amount of matching calico print. If the outer fabric isn't quite heavy enough, you can fuse it to medium-weight Pellon®. Cut a 45-inch-diameter circle of each fabric. Seam the two together with a ¼-inch seam, leaving an 8-inch opening for turning.

After turning and edgestitching the piece, all you have to do is sew a 22-inch separating zipper on the outside. Unzip the zipper and separate it. Lay it along the diameter of the circle so that it forms a straight line

80 THE BIG BAG BOOK

from side to side. Both top or both bottom ends of the zipper should meet at the center of the circle. Sew it flat through all layers. Now, when you slip the ends of the zipper back together and zip it, you will have a cone-shaped bag.

Finish it, as shown, with two pieces of strap, 6 inches and 18 inches long, and a buckle (Chapter 1).

For the picnic-pack circle you will need only 7/8 yard each of two coordinated cotton fabrics. We used heavy piqué. You will also need eight 1-inch plastic rings, a few pieces of elastic, a small cutting board (ours is 7 inches), and 2 yards of heavy cotton cable cord.

Cut two 30-inch circles, seam and edgestitch them as for the yellow bag. Lay the cutting board in the exact center of the inside fabric. Mark lines along the edge of the board, continuing out to the edges of the circle. Stitch along these lines to partition the circle into sides and corners. Sew four 4-inch loops of elastic across the corner of the square which is marked out for the board. Sew straps or pockets, as you like, to the side panels for silver, napkins, wine, anything you want to carry.

Sew the rings firmly by hand at the end of each row of stitching. Run the cable cord through all the rings and knot the ends together.

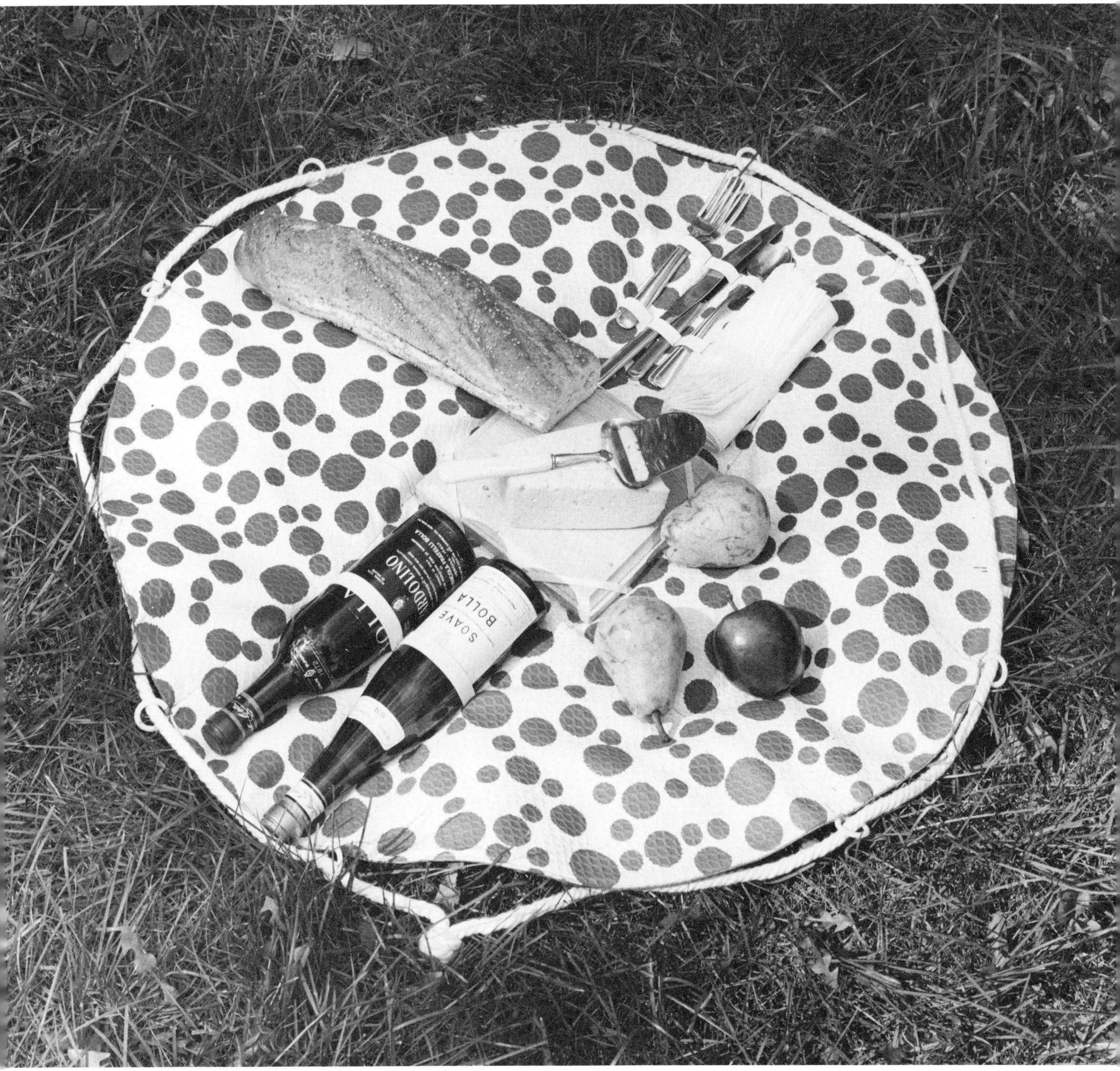
SOAVE
BOLLA

9

Have Bag - Will Travel

Whether it's for a week in the car, coast-to-coast, or a weekend by plane, luggage is lighter, more casual, and easier to "carry on, carry off." It's made to roll up, fold up, hang from the shoulder, and push into crowded corners of overpacked cars. Big tote bags have replaced suitcases for the crowd who weekends in the country. Knit dresses and knit shirts slip into the zip pockets of a roll-up, and the casual jackets stay right in the hanger bag they live in at home.

We planned a coordinated, easy-to-store, his-and-hers set of travel bags which can undergo a lot of changes and modifications to suit your own way of life. Of course, you can add matching tote bags and convertible backpacks to meet any and every traveling need. The sturdy durable fabrics are practical and not too expensive and the construction is mostly flat and simple. The fold-ups and roll-ups are all planned on the same basic principle, which is open to endless variations, plate 7.

1. The big roll-up carries all the shirts, underwear, socks, or any other items that are easy to fold, for a weekend or a couple of weeks. We've shown its development and how it looks and works finished. From these four-step directions you should find the shoe bag and cosmetic bag a simple follow-up.

a. Cut a rectangle 48 inches x 20 inches of firm denim outer fabric, heavy Pellon®, and sturdy cotton-plaid drapery fabric. Lay the Pellon® on the wrong side of the denim and cover it with the plaid lining. Stitch the layers together around the edge. Use a 2-yard piece of webbing, make a circle of it, and stitch it in place as a wraparound handle, covering half the length of the denim, as shown. Cut two pockets 14½ inches x 20 inches and two pockets 10½ inches x 20 inches and sew an 18-inch zipper at the top of each one.

b. Lay one large pocket wrong side down on the lining at the handle end of the bag and stitch it in place. Lay a small pocket right side down over it and stitch it in place along the upper zipper tape of the first pocket. Turn it up, stitch the sides in place, and lay the next pocket right side down over it. If you're nervous about the length

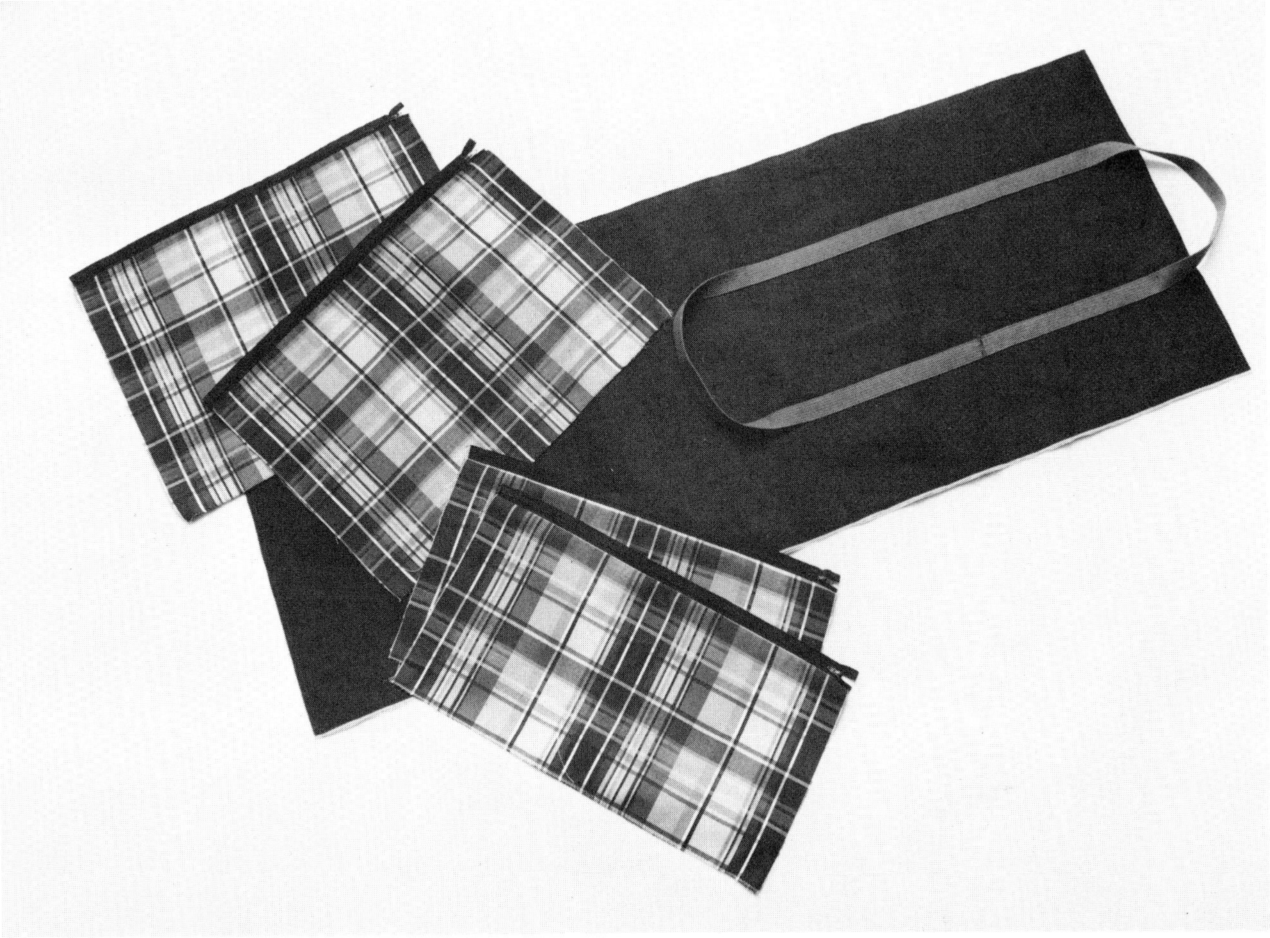

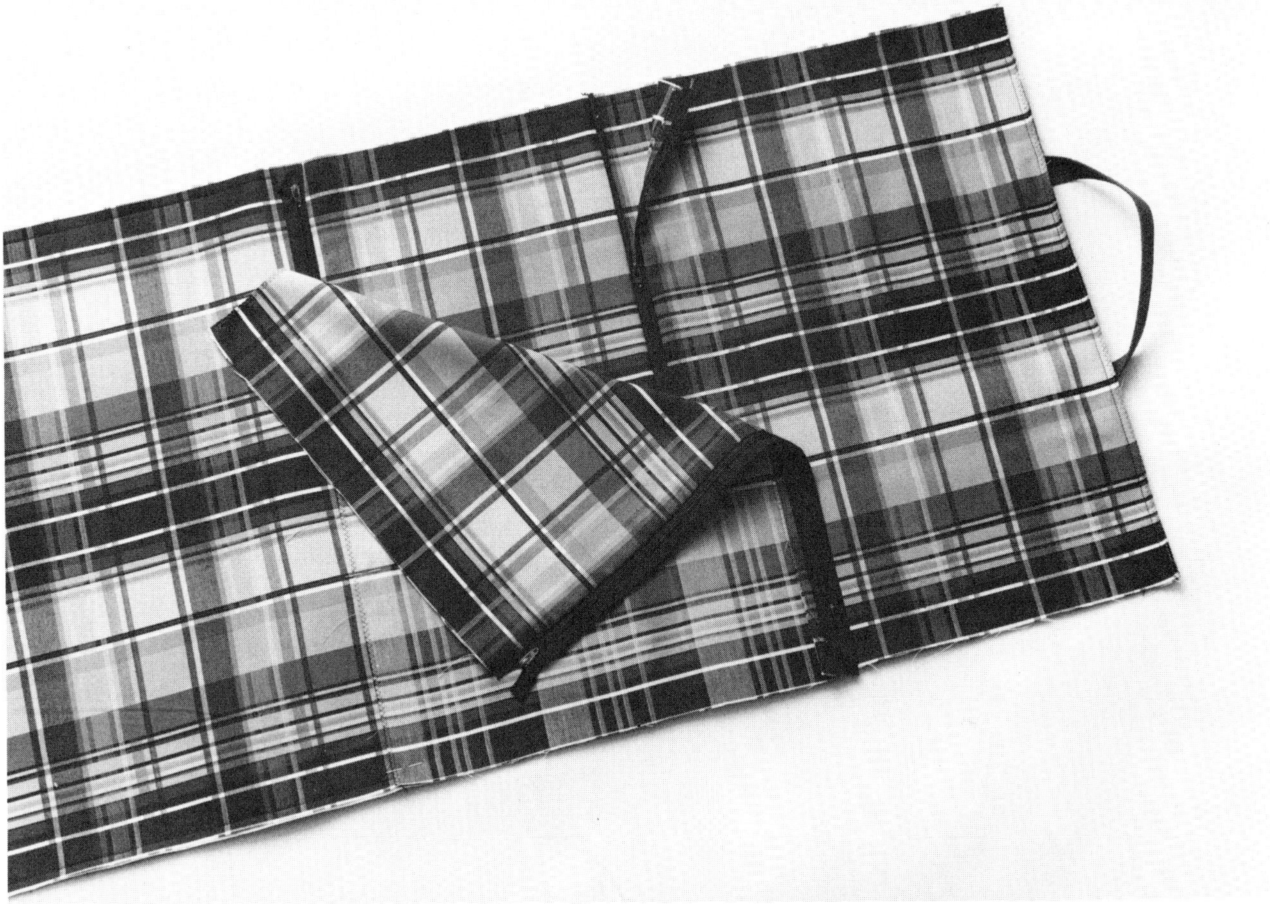

coming out right, you can pin the pockets one after the other along one edge as a trial run, then unpin them to stitch one at a time.

c. Stitch the upper zipper tape of the last pocket to the edge and bind the entire piece with wide bias binding, 1 inch (Chapter 1).

d. Fold the bag over twice from the end without handles, pick up both handles, and you're on your way.

2. The cosmetic bag is made almost like the big roll-up in miniature. We used heavy red canvas for the outside, a decorative layer of red-and-white polka-dot calico, and a layer of medium-weight, pliable, transparent plastic sheeting. The plastic is carried by the yard in houseware departments in several weights; see directions for synthetic leathers and handle it the same way (Chapter 1).

a. Cut rectangles, 23 inches x 11 inches, of all three fabrics. Lay the decorative lining wrong sides together with the canvas and stitch the edges together. Lay the plastic over the lining and paper-clip it in place.

Cut 3 yards of 2-inch-wide bias from the lining fabric. Cut three pockets of the plastic, 8 inches x 11 inches, 10 inches x 11 inches, and 6 inches x 11 inches. Finish the upper edge of the 8-inch pocket with binding (Chapter 1). Finish the upper ends of the other two pockets with 10-inch zippers. Lay the bound pocket at the bottom end of the rectangle and stitch it at the edges through all layers. Seam the 10-inch pocket right side down 1½ inches above the edge of the first pocket. Fold it so that it forms a pleat for expansion at the bottom and stitch the edges in place through all layers. Sew the last pocket in place right side down over the upper zipper tape of the second pocket.

b. Finish the edges with binding. Use the remaining bias to make two ties. Stitch one in place in the space at the top of the bound pocket and one on the upper end.

3. The fold-up shoe carrier is made of firm denim, without either lining or interfacing. We needed 4 yards of wide (1-inch) bias, 2 yards of narrow double-fold, and 2 yards of webbing for the handles.

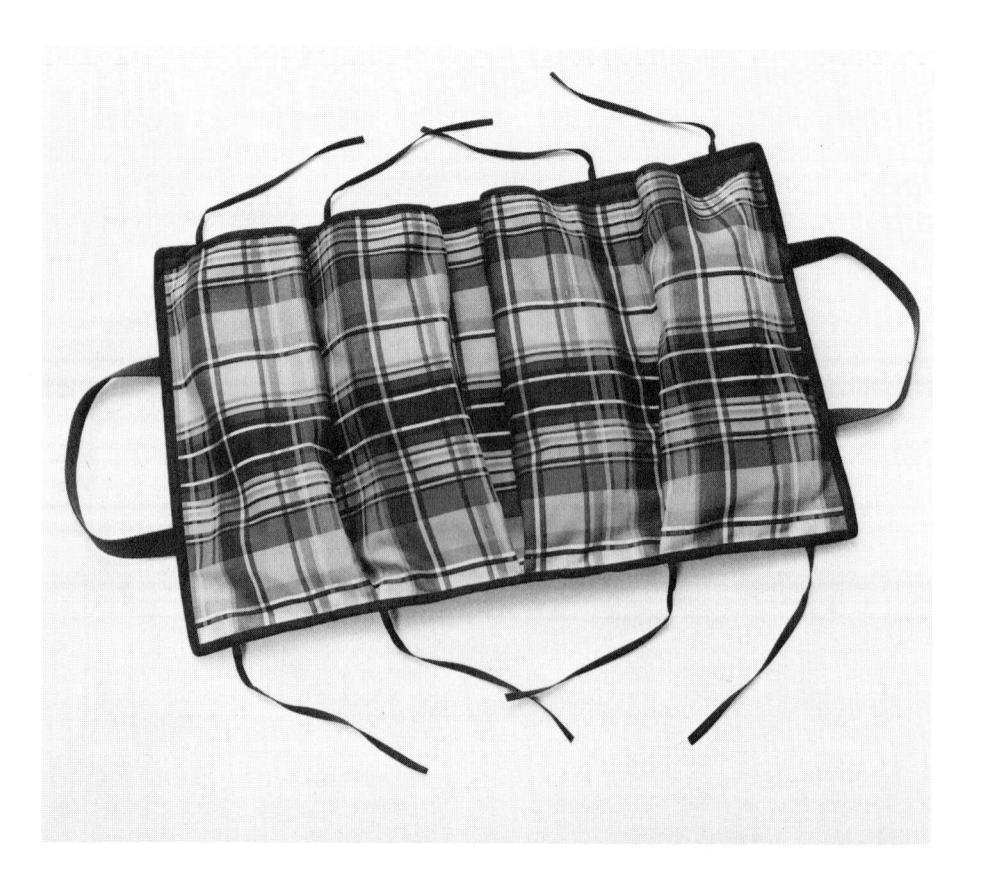

a. Cut a 26-inch-x-18-inch piece of denim and a 38-inch-x-17-inch piece of sturdy lining fabric for the pockets. Make a circle of the 2 yards of webbing and stitch it for a wraparound handle to the outside of the bag. Bind one long edge of the pocket rectangle.

Mark off one long edge of the denim rectangle into spaces of 6 inches at each end, then 5½ inches, and then a center section of 3 inches, which will be the bottom of the bag when it is closed. Mark the pocket piece into 9-inch sections at each end, then 8½ inches, and then 3 inches at the center. Pin the marked points of the raw edge of the pocket piece to the marked points on one edge of the denim. Stitch a line all the way across from each point, backstitching at the bound edge of the pocket.

Fold each pocket in a pleat toward the center until the three raw edges of the two rectangles lie together. Stitch the edges and then bind them. Make ties of the double-fold bias and sew them in place along the edges, as shown.

b. This bag will carry four pairs of ladies' shoes, two in a pocket, or two pairs of men's singly. If you are planning for low boots or very large or heavy shoes, increase the length of the rectangles, thereby increasing the capacity of the pockets.

4. The hanger bag is very personal in that it must fit the width of your hangers, the length of your clothes, and be deep enough to accom-

modate as many pieces as you want. We are giving you the dimensions that we used, which will carry two suits or jackets for a medium-size man. We also decided to zip the boxing strip instead of the center front. If you want it the other way, you can cut one front panel in two pieces, adding seam allowances for the zipper, and cut the boxing strip all in one.

Our finished bag is 20 inches across, 36 inches long and 3 inches deep. We used two packs of wide (1-inch) bias binding and a 22-inch zipper. You may be able to find a longer zipper in a home-decorating department.

We cut the side pieces 20 inches x 36 inches plus a little allowance for outside bound seams. We left an area 1½ inches wide at the center top and cut the shoulder slant down from that point to conform to the shape of the hangers. We also rounded the bottom corners for easier binding. We cut two 24-inch-x-2¼-inch zipper strips and a pieced boxing strip 3½ inches x 72 inches (a little too long but easy to remedy).

Set the zipper between the two strips and narrowly hem the upper end (open end of the zipper). Narrowly hem the flat places at the top of the sides and one end of the boxing strip. Pin the boxing strip and the zipper strip in place, wrong sides together with the bag sides, letting all of the narrowly hemmed spots form a small opening for the necks of the hangers. Stitch the strips in place ¼ inch from the raw edges, cutting off the boxing strip at the end as needed, and seaming it to the zipper strip. Finish the edges with bias binding (Chapter 1).

Make a small strap tab to close over the end of the zipper. Sew it in place at the neck and fasten it with a gripper or square of Velcro®.

In retailoring this hanger bag to fit your own needs, remember to plan for seams along the zipper in one of the two places mentioned. Always cut the boxing strip too long, rather than too short. Allow enough extra width over the hanger size and the length of the garments so that the garments are not crushed.

5. A thin, strong case that can be tucked in the corner of a larger bag is especially useful to travelers who shop along the way. We kept

ours light by not lining or interfacing it and made it strong by using very sturdy denim and cording the seams.

This is a simple boxed bag, with corners rounded for easy seaming (page 31). Cut two rectangles 17 inches x 14 inches, a boxing strip 5 inches x 37 inches, and two zipper strips 3 inches x 23 inches (seams included on all). Round the corners of the rectangles—this will make the boxing strip a little too long, but as you know, that's no problem. We used a 22-inch zipper and 1¼ yards of 1-inch-wide webbing cut in two pieces.

You can buy corded piping already made up or make your own from bias scraps cut 1½ inches wide and pieced. Fold it over small cable cord, wrong sides together, and stitch with a zipper foot. Install it along the seamline of the bag side pieces, on the right side of the fabric, and with all raw edges in the same direction, using the zipper foot.

Sew the zipper in place between the strips and the handles in place near the upper edge of each side of the bag. Assemble the pieces as described for boxed bags (page 31), again using the zipper foot along the piped seams.

10

Treasured Playthings

Everybody's treasures need a special place of their own. It doesn't matter whether you are ten or a hundred, whether your treasures are silver and gold or jacks and marbles. It's especially nice to have a bag to fit if you like to take your favorite belongings visiting with you. Names and identifications on them make them very personal.

The big red toy carrier will hold a lot of things. It and the yellow one, cover, are alike and have the advantage of being rigid so that trucks and tanks and teddy bear are all at home in them. The smaller bags have simple lettering applied, the identification of the contents on one side and the owner's name on the other, plate 12.

Any of the totes, duffles, and many other basic bags can be scaled down and converted for toy use. Easy-care fabrics are a good idea for the little ones that get carried around a lot. It's better not to go to too great expense or to the trouble of linings and handwork. The important thing is the finished effect, especially if you are giving the marble or jacks bag as a gift, already properly filled. A friend once said that if there was anything that her children liked on a gift, it was a picture of their grubby little faces or their name in bold letters.

Before we talk about making the bags, we'd like to discuss quick ways of lettering. Of course you can make machine monograms and initials, as described in Chapter 15. We felt even that was a lot of work and that entire words and names were more fun. So we resorted to the quick, cheap, and fun tricks in Chapter 16. That means that we used a stencil alphabet from the local variety store. Letters ¾ inch or 1 inch high are about right and they can be applied with paint, crayon, or iron-on mending fabric (page 136). The letters on the dolly duffle are made of double-folded bias binding stitched on by machine, a totally free-hand operation.

1 & 2. Both the jacks and the marbles bags are made like the flat bag with handles (page 26), except that an opening is left in the side seam near the top, where the hem forms a casing, so that cord can be run in. Cut one long strip of fabric, from 6 inches to 8 inches wide and from 14 inches to 18 inches long, or two short pieces that add up to the same size. Plan the placement of the letters so that all of the name goes on one side and the identification on the other. We like the letters sort of wandering at random. Apply them before sewing the side seams and the hem. We used the cut-off legs of old jeans and a nifty denim-look braided cord for the marble bag. The jacks bag is of unbleached muslin with the same sort of cord in off-white.

3. The dimensions of the dolly duffle have to fit the dolly that you have in mind, plus enough room to pack her clothes in around her. The general directions for duffles (page 30) will help in cutting and assembling. We used a firm canvas and so were able to omit interfacing and

finished with outside bound seams (Chapter 1), so a lining was not necessary. The handles and binding are made of wide (1-inch) calico printed bias binding and the letters of matching double-fold bias, one pack of each. We used a 10-inch zipper.

Cut circles with a 5¾-inch diameter for the ends, and a rectangle of 12-inches x 18 inches. These measurements include the necessary ⅜-inch outside seam. Cut 48 inches of the wide bias for wraparound handles. Back the actual handle parts with 1-inch-wide ribbon—less than 1 yard.

4. The rigid carrier is actually useful for lots of things besides toys, including sports equipment and picnics. We think it makes an ideal way for a small person to travel with his most treasured possessions, in the car or on a train or plane. Here are step-by-step directions for the way we did it, using a firm plastic bucket that looks just like a wooden peach basket. Any medium-size plastic trash basket will work. We used three yards of braid, 2 inches wide, soft enough to ease around the curves.

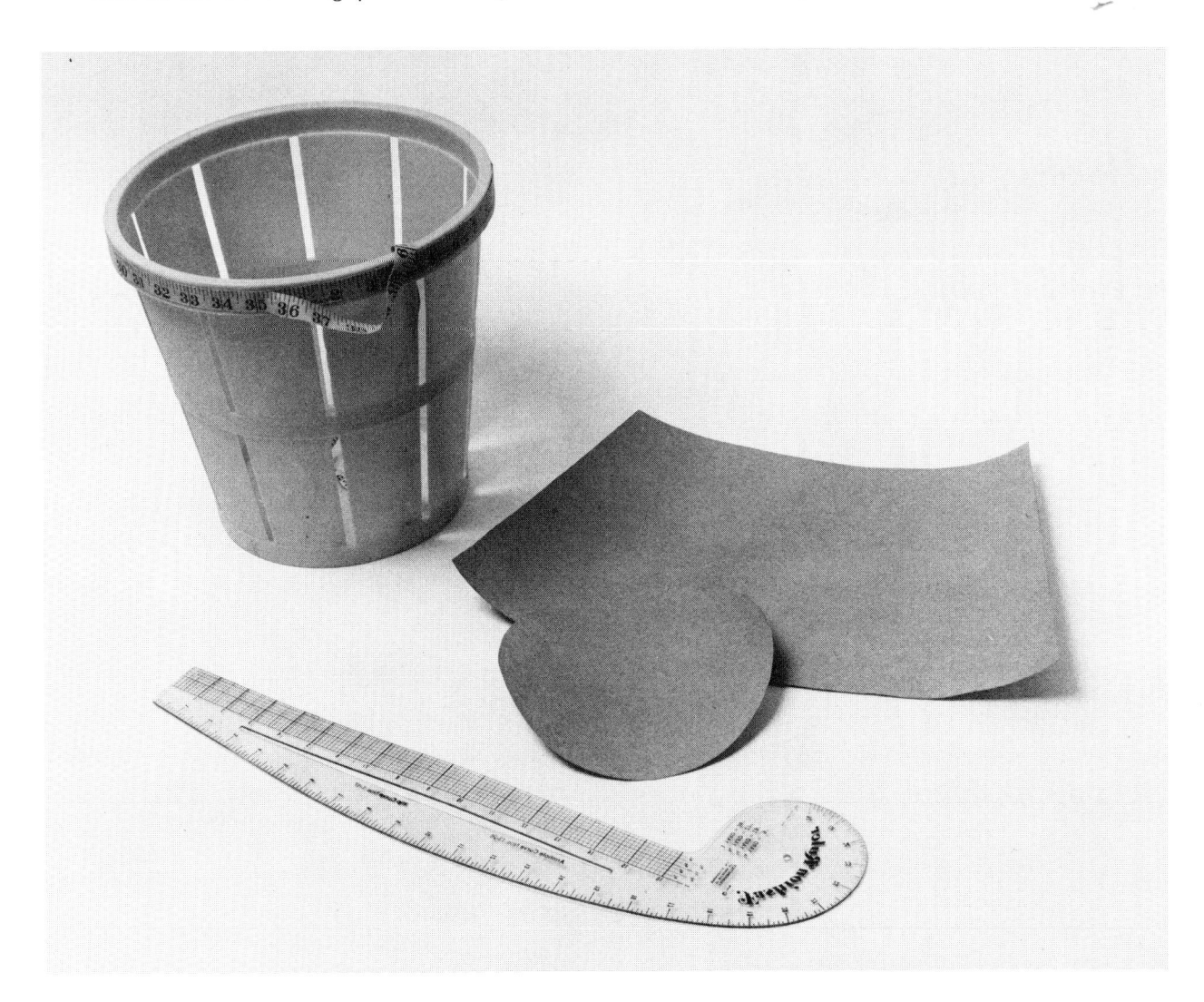

a. Measure the height of the basket and the circumference of both the top and bottom. Allow a little extra to make it easy to slip the basket in and out. Draw a brown-paper pattern for the bottom and half of the side, using your drafting tools. Recheck the side piece against the basket until you get the shape the way you want it. If you cut the side piece double in muslin, you can try it on before cutting into your good fabric.

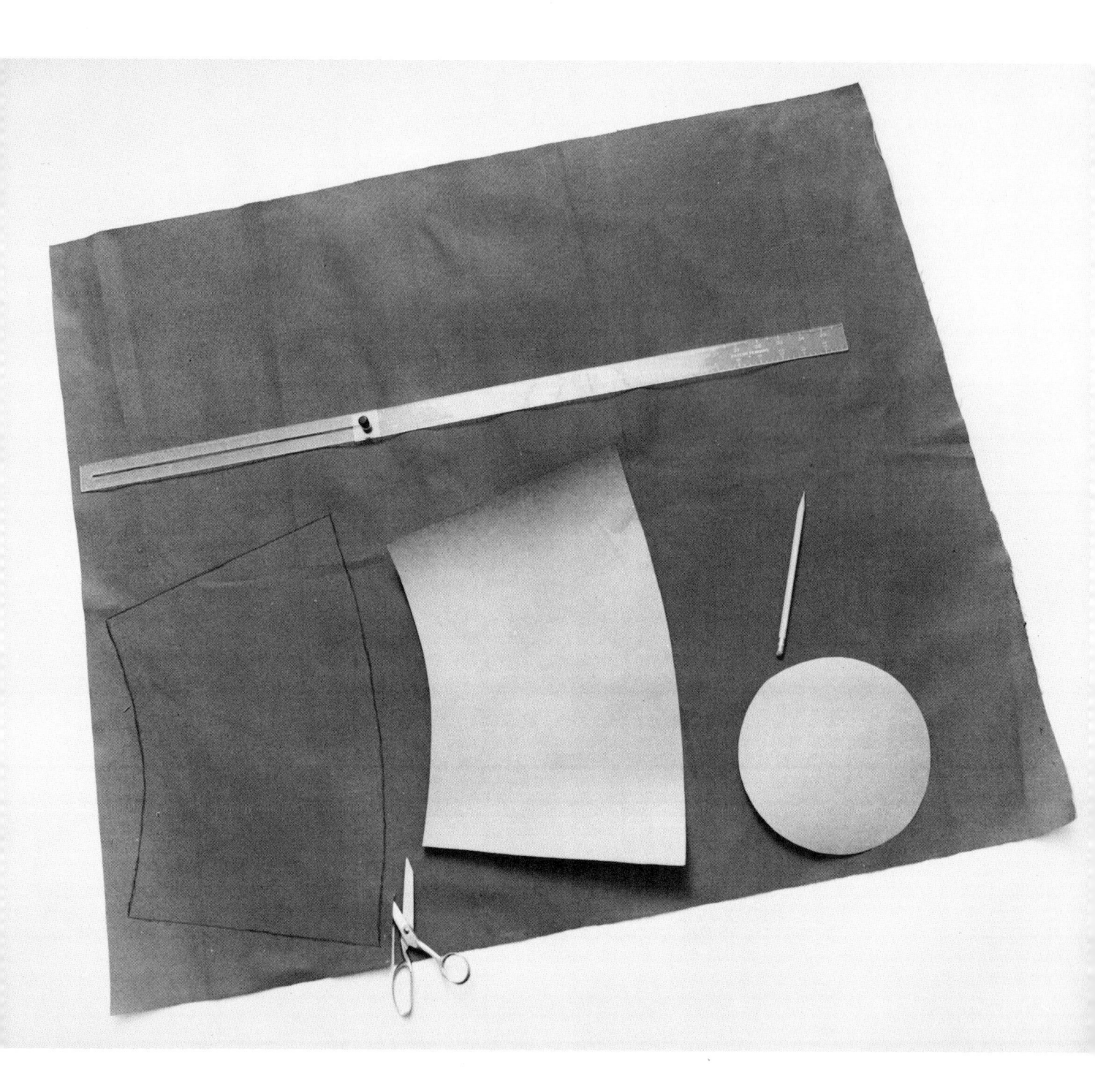

b. The basket we used needed about 1⅛ yards of canvas, either 36 inches or 45 inches wide. Lay the pattern pieces as shown and draw around them. Cut the upper cuff piece about 9 inches deep and the

Treasured Playthings 95

length of the circumference of the top of the basket, allowing enough for end seams. If you have made your brown-paper-pattern pieces seamless, remember to cut ½ inch outside of them, too.

c. A flat assembly method is easier for most of the stitching. Seam the side pieces together along one side. Join the long raw edge of the cuff piece wrong sides together with the side piece. Stitch the longer or upper edge of each strip of braid in place first. Ease the lower edge, using an ease thread if you wish, or steaming the braid in shape before stitching. Cut six loops of braid, 7 inches long. Plan for two to cover the top ends of the side seams and the others to be evenly spaced between. Sew all but one in place, on the wrong side and then over to the right, as shown.

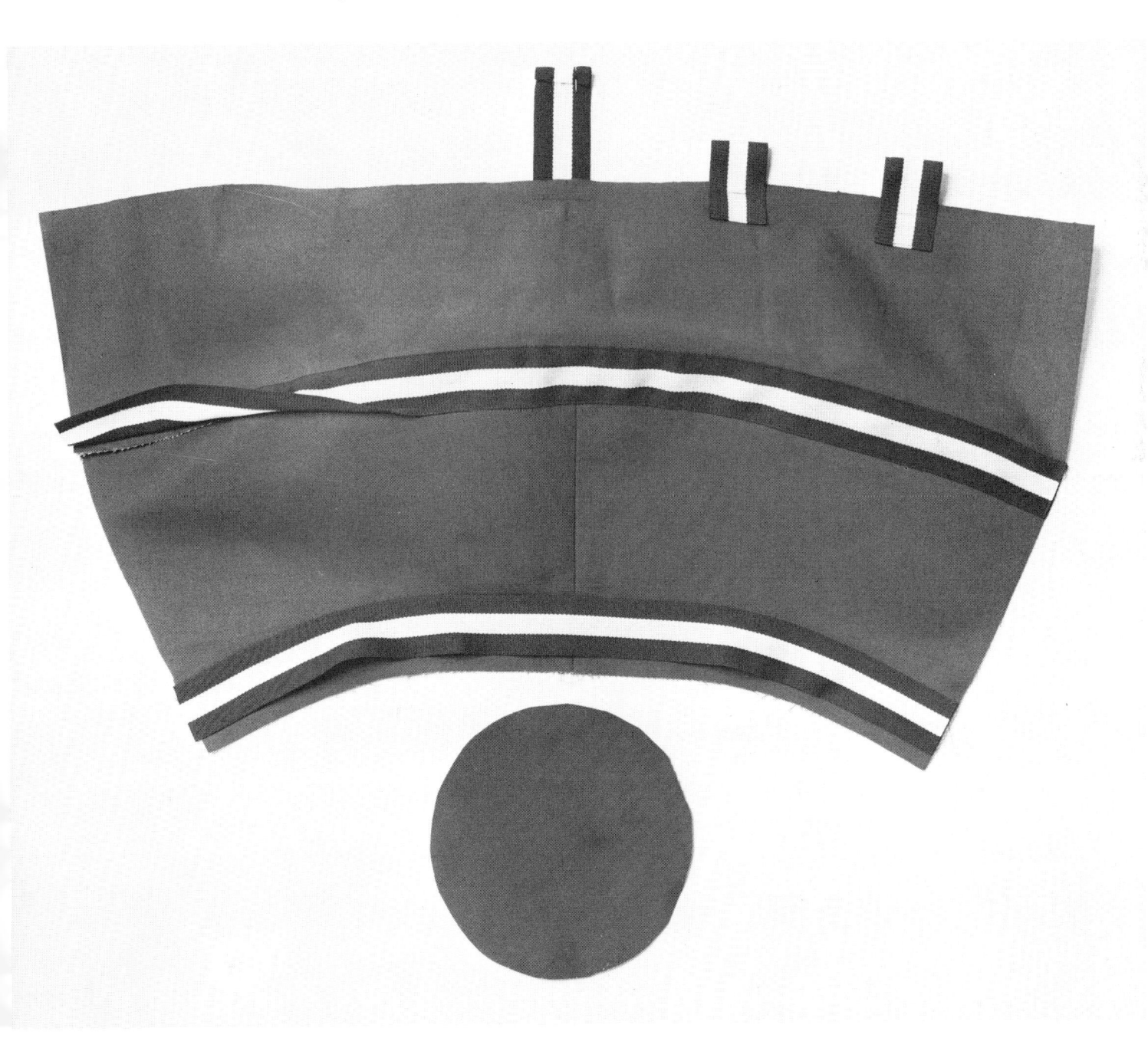

d. The last step is the hardest. Seam the last side of the large piece and sew the last loop over the top end of that seam. Mark and pin the large piece in place, right sides together with the circle. Look at round bags (page 29) for help in marking and clipping. When you machine stitch this last seam, you may find it easier to use the zipper foot to avoid the bump formed by the braid and to stitch as close to the braid as possible. A little over a yard of cable cord will fit around the top.

11

Store It Softly

Bags for storing household equipment and some personal possessions should be useful rather than highly ornamental. Usually they should be roomy, made of soft protective fabrics, and have a tight closing. The easiest styles are foldover bags, drawstring bags, and bags that snap together with Velcro®.

We will not give exact directions or dimensions for these, as everyone's needs will vary. There are a few tips that make it easier, and we'll include directions for the pocketed foldovers, which can be made in any size. It is mostly a matter of measuring carefully and leaving plenty of room for whatever is to go in the storage bag.

98   THE BIG BAG BOOK

Pacific Silvercloth is available (see page 151) and is perfect for making tarnish-proof bags for silver and jewelry or for lining such bags. We made one for a very large ladle that had never had a proper home before. It is a simple flat bag with a 1-inch hem casing and a drawstring. We measured the width, length, and thickness of the ladle and added a couple of inches for good measure. The double bag that holds the children's cups is a flat bag closed at the top with Velcro®. We stitched down the center to keep the two cups apart. The cups were each 10½ inches around, including handles. We made the bag 23 inches around or 11½ inches on each side.

Shoe bags are flat bags with drawstrings and should be made in pairs so that each shoe is protected from rubbing on the other one. Knits, especially cotton knits, are ideal fabrics for them. Dimensions for shoe bags vary greatly with size and style. We can only suggest that finished sizes of 10 inches x 5 inches, 12 inches x 6 inches, and 14 inches x 7 inches will cover most women's and men's conventional shoes. Measure for boots, hightops, bulky platforms, and so on. Since you can make a flat drawstring bag in about twenty minutes and since anyone who sews often has leftover knits, it's easy to make shoe bags for everyone in the family.

Foldbags come in two styles, besides the zippered ones in Chapter 9 —the flat envelope fold and the pocketed fold. The flat envelope is nice for linens and large pieces of lingerie. The one shown here is sized for table mats, 14 inches x 19 inches folded, with a slight adjustment on the Velcro® strap fastenings. Cut two pieces of fabric, 35 inches x 20 inches, and one piece of Pellon® Fleece the same size. Back one piece of fabric with the interfacing and seam the two pieces of fabric right sides together, leaving an opening for turning. Trim the interfacing close to the seams, clip the corners, and turn the piece right sides out. Slipstitch the opening together and stitch two rows of braid lengthwise on the outside. Let the braid extend over one end. Apply two pieces of Velcro®, long to short pieces (page 71), to allow for slight adjustment in the envelope flap.

The trick to the pocketed foldbag is to plan pleats in one layer of the fabric, which form pockets when the edges are stitched in place to the other layer. For a 3-inch-deep pocket, plan 9 inches for pleat; for a 4-inch plan 12 inches. Allow $\frac{1}{2}$ inch at the bottom for seam and then start marking the pleats. For instance, on the 4-inch pleat, mark $\frac{1}{2}$ inch for seam, then 4 inches, then 8 inches, 4 inches again, and 8 inches again; leave another 4 inches at the top for the envelope flap. Pleat the mark at the top of the 4-inch section up to the 8-inch mark, repeat with the two marks above, and you have two pockets 4 inches deep. Stitch along the sides to secure the pleats and then seam the pleated piece right sides together with a $12\frac{1}{2}$-inch piece, leaving an opening, and turning. If you wish to divide one or both pockets, you can stitch down the center. We used Pacific Silvercloth for the pocket part of the jewelry foldbag.

There are many variations on these bags, depending on your own needs. Some, such as the shoe bag and jewelry foldbags, are nice for traveling. You can also make zippered small bags using the plans for travel foldbags in Chapter 9. Storage bags make beautiful gifts for the person who has everything and needs a place to keep it.

12

Practical Purses

There may be some question as to what defines a purse or makes it different from any other bag. Many women carry smaller or more decorative tote bags instead of purses, some carry flat bags that double as briefcases, and some stuff everything into their pockets. The word "purse" may denote something vaguely Victorian to twentieth-century women.

We felt, however, that there is a time and a costume which demands a purse. A smart suit or a classic wool dress or a pretty summer cotton can each walk out a little more stylishly with the right purse. If you're on your way to a job interview, or the theater, or your in-laws' for dinner, it may be the time to discard that beloved and well-worn tote bag for something more feminine.

Purses can be large or small, hung over the shoulder, carried on the arm, or clutched in the hand. We have several choices, from strictly tailored to ridiculously frilly, but each quite practical for its specific time. Again, we want you to think of them as suggestions only. Change the fabrics, the trimmings, the sizes.

1. Convertible bags, to be carried over the shoulder or with a shortened strap on the arm, can be made in two sizes from our pattern. Use the pattern as is, adding seams all around on each piece, or double the size for a roomy businesslike bag, plate 3.

For the small bag we used only ¼ yard of heavy brown poplin, scraps of heavy Pellon® and cotton-print lining, 4 yards of 1-inch-wide decorative cotton braid, a 7-inch invisible zipper, and two small tortoise-shell rings. We cut two side pieces, the boxing strip (adding seams), and two strips 8 inches x 1¾ inches (including seams) from all three layers of fabric.

Machine baste the fabric sides onto the Pellon®, draw a diagonal line for the first row of braid, and start stitching. Measure an even distance and mark for the next row. Cover both sides. Incorporate the lining with all pieces (Chapter 1).

Insert the zipper between the two straight strips. Seam that piece along the top curve of both side panels—stop the stitching ½ inch from the ends and backstitch. Leaving the zipper open for turning, seam the

FOLD

FOLD

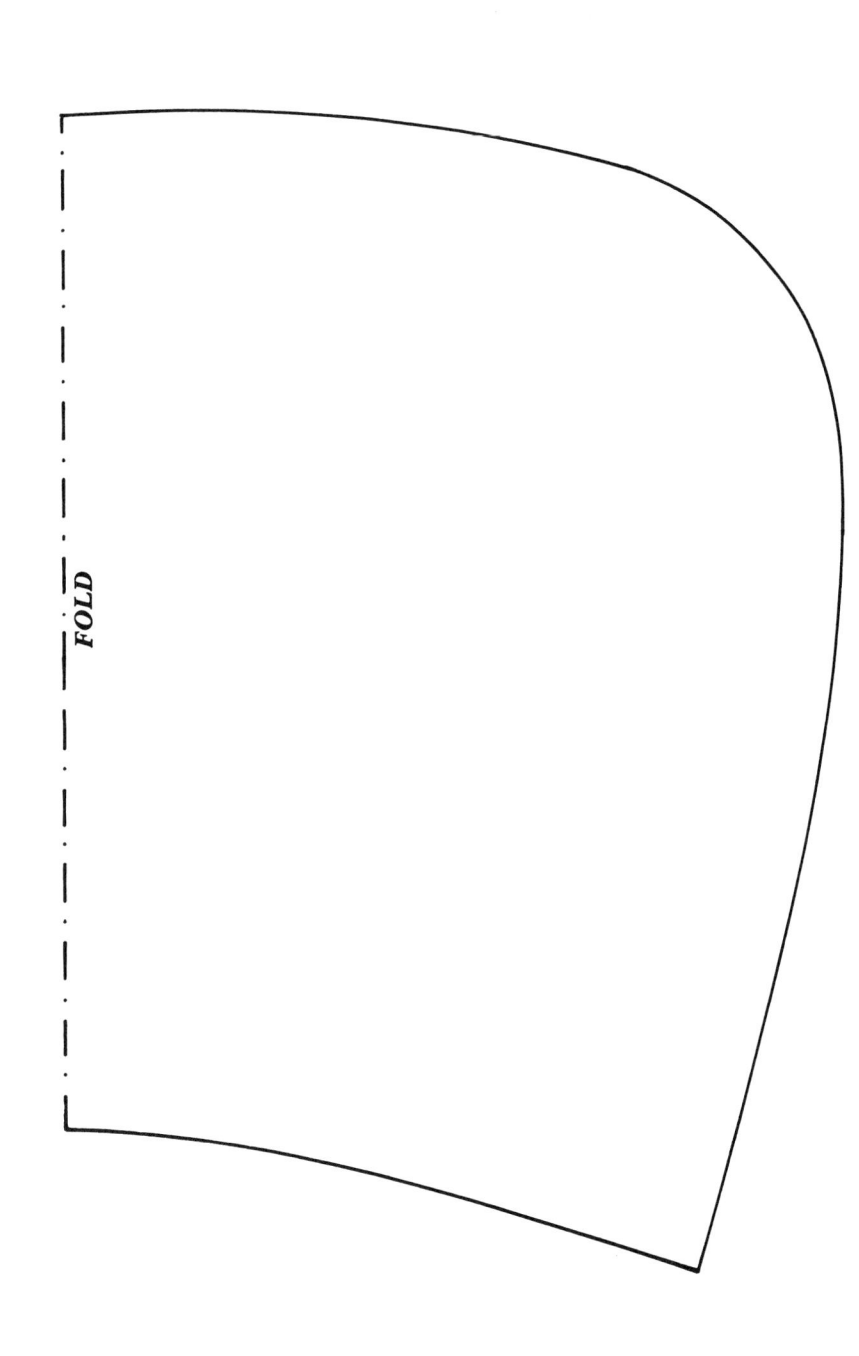

Full-size pattern.
Add seams.

FOLD

boxing strip around the rest of the bag, again stopping and backstitching ½ inch before the ends.

Cut two 4-inch pieces of the braid, fold them wrong sides together through the rings. Insert the raw ends of each doubled piece of braid into the space left at the corners between the boxing strip and the zipper strip. Pin in place and seam across, running the stitching back and forth for security. If this creates too much of a struggle with the machine, it can be done quite easily by hand with a heavy needle and double thread. Turn the bag right side out.

You should have enough braid left to make a double-layered strap, 24 inches to 26 inches long. Run twice that length of braid through one ring, turn the raw ends in toward each other, pin the layers together, and edgestitch them. Fold a 2-inch end of the completed strap through the other ring, mark meeting points, and sew Velcro® to hold it in place. Sew another piece of Velcro® on the under side of the handle almost back to the other ring so that the end of the strap can also be fastened all the way back, making it short enough for an arm purse.

The larger purse is made in exactly the same way. We used about ⅝ yard of a heavy tan twill-weave cotton. The sides are interfaced with Pellon® Fleece to make the diagonal quilting look deeper. The quilting is stitched along the lines of the twill weave for easy accuracy. The strap handle is made of a yard of 1½-inch-wide tan webbing, but could be cut of fabric if no matching webbing can be found. The large wooden rings are from David Traum, available at notions counters. We made the strap single and hemmed one end around one ring and made a 2-inch hem on the free end. We used grippers instead of Velcro® to make the strap adjustable.

2. We think that Ultrasuede® was practically invented for bag makers who don't want to work in real leather. It is beautiful, supple, colorful, and washable. It is expensive, but as you can see, the tiniest scraps can be used effectively. It might be possible to work out trades with friends who sew to get it at the best price of all—free, plate 2.

Both clutch purses are interfaced with medium-weight Pellon®. The striped purse is made exactly like the flat denim one (page 27). The dimensions of the Pellon® base, onto which the stripes are stitched, is 9 inches x 11 inches. The stripes are 2 inches wide—no seams are needed, as Ultrasuede® doesn't ravel. We used the widest zigzag on the machine to set the stripes close together—no overlap. They could also be stitched on with a straight stitch. The purse is completed like the flat denim bag. We omitted the strap handle but it could be made of a layer of Ultrasuede® sewed to a narrow grosgrain ribbon.

For pure whimsy we suggest a clutch purse with a drawing of your own hand for decoration. Just trace around it on paper to make a pattern. We backed the 11-inch-x-16-inch piece of Ultrasuede® with the Pellon® before stitching the hand in place with a straight stitch about 1/16 inch from the edge of the design. We joined the seams with outside double-stitching, in the manner of real suede. The top of the bag is made sturdier by an extra 1-inch band of Ultrasuede® stitched along the zipper. The lining is set in by hand.

A few words about Ultrasuede®—you can use a warm iron on it over a transparent press cloth, so fusing is possible. See Chapter 1 for synthetic leather tips.

3. If you don't use purses every day but want one once in a while, the slipcover bag is for you. It can change colors and seasons faster than a chameleon. We based ours on the summer version because the inner bag had to conform to the width of the decorative braid, which is 2½ inches wide. That means that all width measurements are multiples of that.

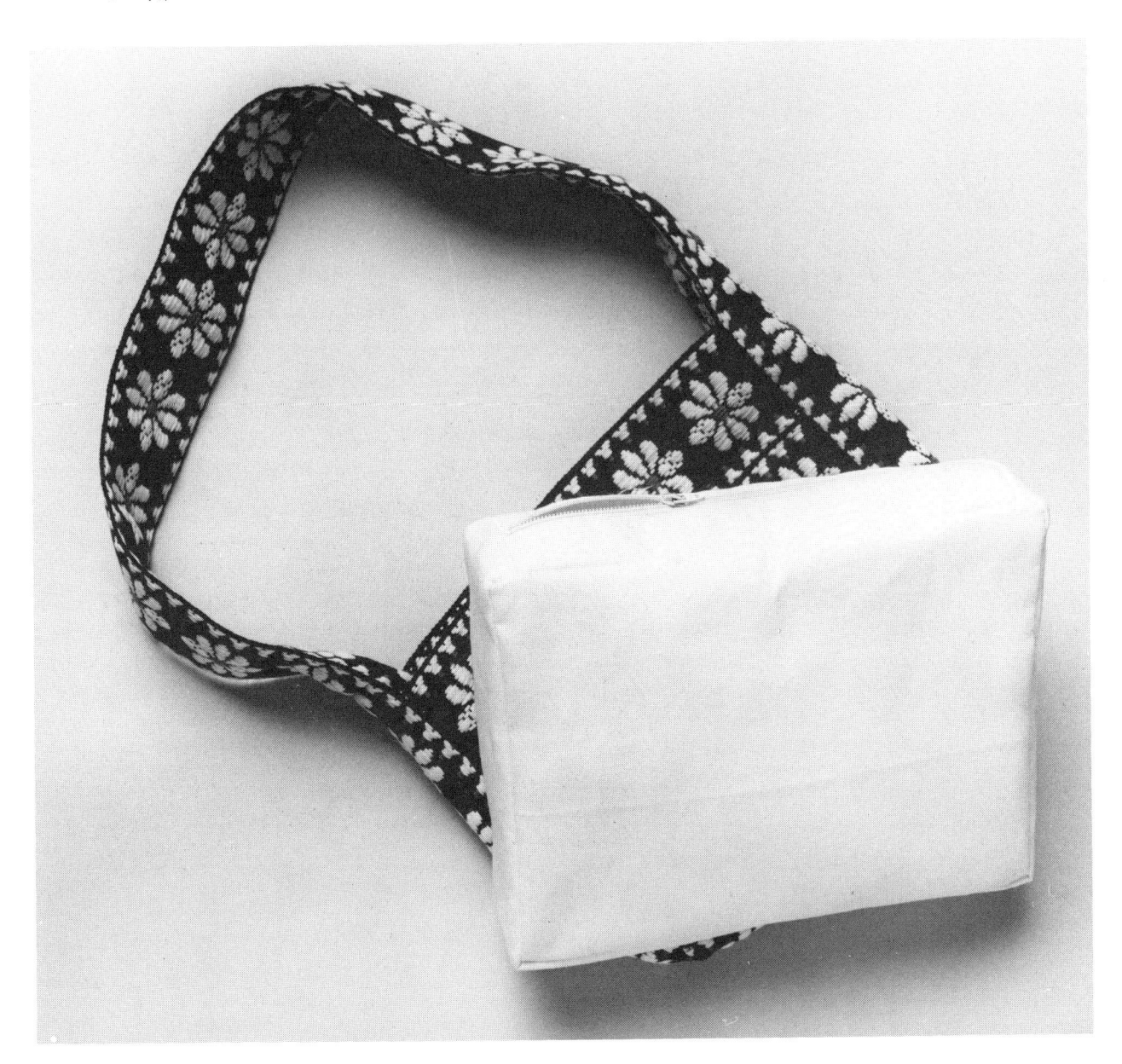

a. The inner bag is made of plain white linen-weave cotton, interfaced with heavy Pellon® and lined with cotton sateen. The zipper is 10 inches. We cut two side panels 8½ inches x 11 inches, a boxing strip 3½ inches x 26 inches, and two zipper strips 2¾ inches x 11 inches (seams included on all pieces). All pieces were cut again in each fabric and layered. We then assembled the bag like the boxed bags (page 31). We made the seams a tiny fraction wider than the allowed ½ inch so that the bag would be small enough to slip inside the cover.

b. To be on the safe side, buy 4 yards of decorative braid so that you can match bold patterns as we did. Cut six 11-inch strips for the sides, and stitch them edge-to-edge with a wide zigzag. If you have only a straight-stitch machine, place a piece of cotton-twill tape under the joining and stitch each edge of the braid to it. The boxing strip is 26 inches long. Stitch it along the bottom of both side pieces to a point ½ inch short of each raw end of the side pieces. Turn up the ends, overlapping the raw section ½ inch, and stitch it in place—there should be ½ inch of boxing strip extending above the top at each end.

Cut a piece about 27 inches for a handle and seam it to the ends of the boxing strip. Cut another piece 14 inches longer, center it wrong sides together with the handle, and stitch the edges of the two together as far as the top of the bag. Finish the longer piece by hand over the raw ends inside.

c. A simple winter cover can be made of wool—plain or plaid—of Ultrasuede®, or of corduroy. For speed make it like a tote bag with

mitered lower corners. That means that you will cut the sides 13½ inches wide, including seams. We cut them 15 inches deep so that the

106 THE BIG BAG BOOK

end folds over and hides the white inner bag. We also made a side pocket 13½ inches x 10 inches. The strap is 2½ inches x 22 inches, backed with a piece of 1½-inch grosgrain ribbon.

Hem the upper edge of the pocket 1 inch and lay the pocket wrong side down to the right side of one bag piece. Pin it in place and incorporate it in the seams. Seam the two sides together and miter the corner 2½ inches. Sew the handles on the sides about 6 inches up from the miters. We finished the upper ends by fringing the wool about 1 inch deep. You may use a decorative braid or trim instead—Ultrasuede® needs no finish.

4. Once in a while the blue jeans are set aside and a girl likes to feel very feminine. A ruffled lacy purse could go anywhere from first communion up to the first prom. This one is made in the same way as the round gathered bag, page 29, but smaller.

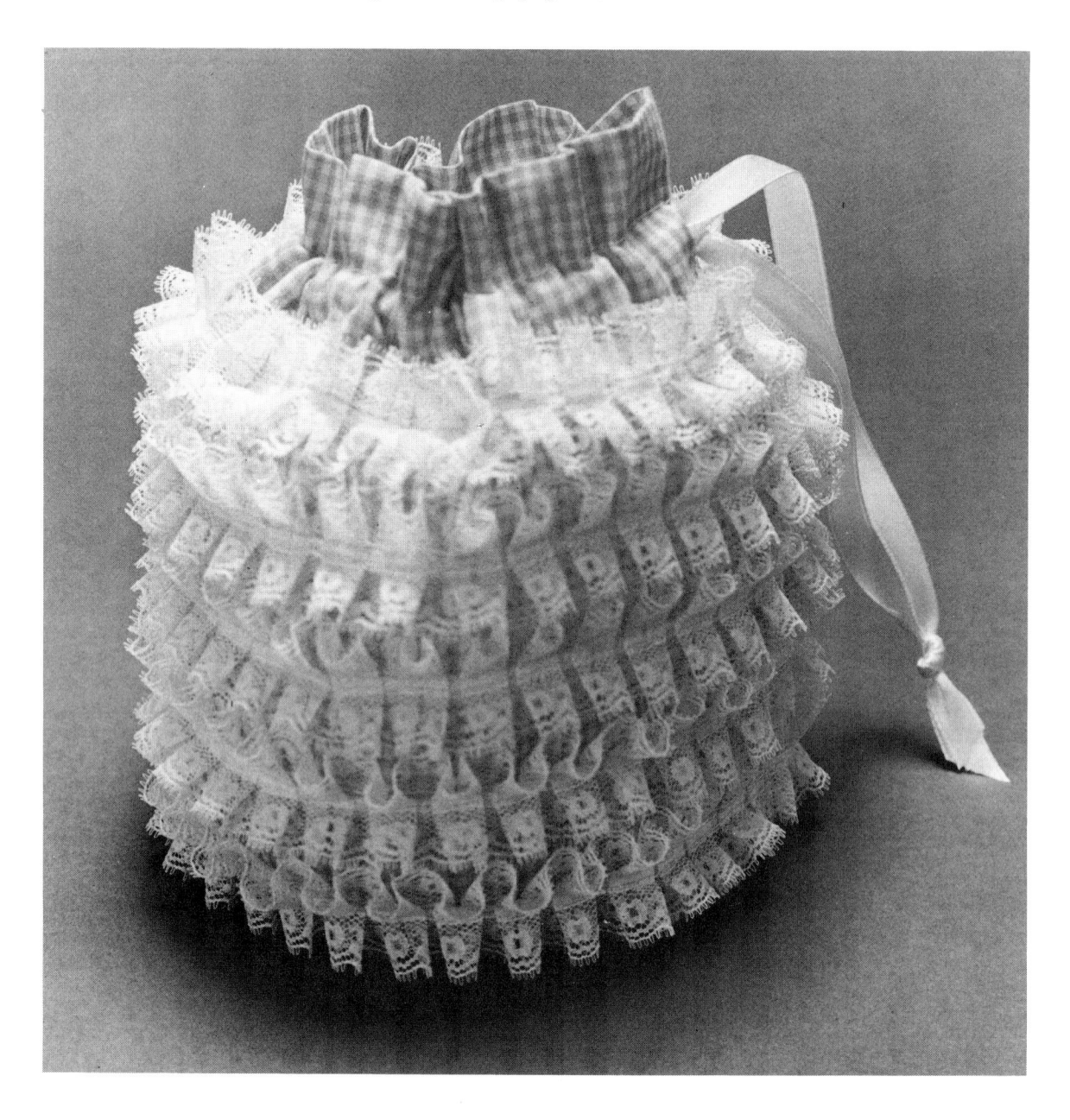

Any semisheer cotton or cotton-blend fabric makes a nice base—we used a delicate pastel checked gingham—mostly because there were enough scraps of it left from a girl's pinafore. You will also need 2½ yards of double-edged lace ruffling, about 1¼ inches wide, and ¾ yards of narrow ribbon.

Cut the bottom 4 inches in diameter (including seams) twice in the fabric and once in heavy Pellon®. Cut the side piece 17 inches x 11 inches. Cut the lace into 17-inch pieces and start about 1½ inches from the lower edge, sewing it in rows very close together. You will have about 3½ inches left at the top for a heading and casing totaling 1½ inches. See Chapter 2.

13

Glitter a Little

What else are evenings for except to get dressed up and go out into the glittering evening world? The plainest black dress or velvet pants suit deserves the sparkle of a tiny evening bag. From the Victorian reticule to the modern tote, every kind of bag gets into the act.

 1. The furoshiki in shimmering silk makes a nice summer-evening bag. Make it by hand, using the directions in Chapter 4. It started life as one of those little silk scarves from Thailand. Once we discovered that it was slightly more than three times as long as it was wide, it was doomed to turn into a furoshiki. We cut off the extra 4 inches of length (which gave us a piece for the gussets), hand hemmed that end, and we were on our way to an almost instant bag, plate 14.

2. Less than ½ yard of gold synthetic leather, the same amount of green-gold silk, a scrap of medium-weight Pellon®, and 2 yards of ½-inch-wide gold braid turned into a glittery but practical tote. Basic directions in Chapters 2 and 3 are all you need to assemble this miniature. Cut the outer fabric and interfacing 10 inches x 20 inches and the lining 3 inches shorter. The miters at the bottom are 2 inches wide. Make ½-inch-wide handles of lining fabric (Chapter 1), and stitch the braid on them. You will use approximately 1⅛ yards of the braid to trim the upper edge of the bag and the upper edge of the lining, so the handles will be cut of what is left. The measurements are not critical and should be based on what you have and what you like, plate 14.

3. If you have a crazy quilt that is wearing out in spots and you've decided to cut it up, you will be well on your way to the little pieced and patched evening bag. All you have to do is cut a piece 8 inches x 16 inches, a lining and interfacing the same, seam the bag, seam the lining, and assemble with 1-inch-wide velvet ribbon trim and handles.

We made up our own patchwork from bits of silk, velvet, and ribbon. If you are planning your own, lay the interfacing down and start placing small irregular geometric pieces of velvet on it. Then add silks, satins, and bits of ribbon until you like the effect. It is best not to turn the edges of the velvet because it is too heavy, so turn under the silks and also use the selvages on the ribbons to cover the raw edges of the velvet. It is necessary to baste all the pieces in place. Use silk thread in the weight of buttonhole twist or DMC Pearl Cotton, size #8, to embroider along all the joining lines. Herringbone or feather stitch are especially suitable, plate 15.

4. The glittery beaded bag is straight from Grandma's attic. Someone back in the flapper era had a ball gown with these medallions on it

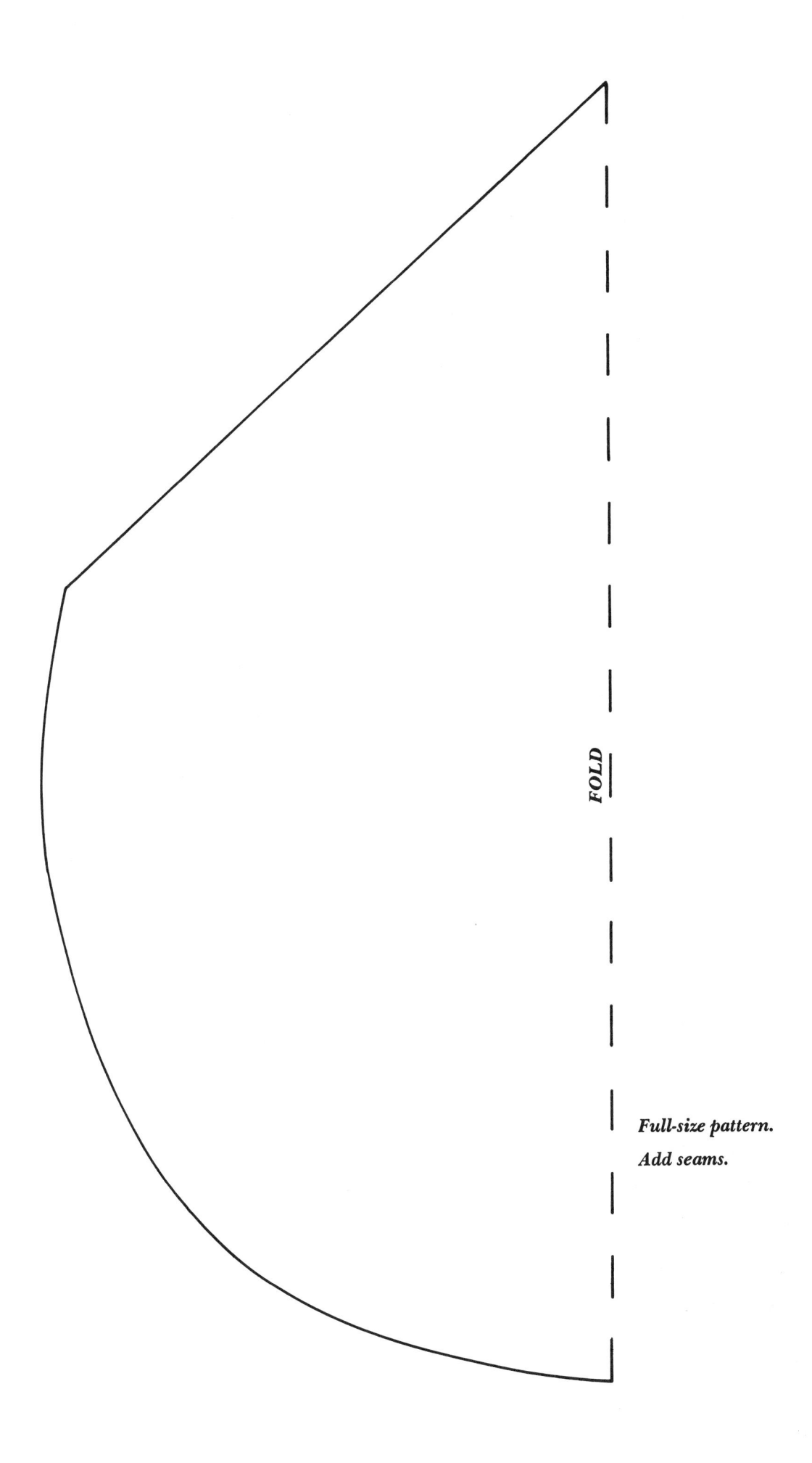

FOLD

Full-size pattern.
Add seams.

and six of them survived to fall into our hands. One day we were looking into a Japanese shop and saw little stiffened silk purses in the very same shape. That solved the problem of what to do with at least two of the medallions. If no one left you such treasures, you can still use the pattern to make a bag of a scrap of velvet or silk brocade. Cover it with beads or braid as you wish.

Because our medallions are of sheer fabric, we basted them to a lightweight lining fabric, leaving a seam allowance on the lining. We cut two pieces of heavy Pellon® and basted those pieces onto them (three layers in all for each side). Then we blindstitched the medallions to the other layers all around the edges. Even with all those beads we found it possible to machine seam the bag pieces together around the curved edge by using the zipper foot.

Make a silk lining like the bag. Use ½-inch-wide decorative braid or ribbon for two loop handles big enough to get your hand through. Attach the handles and finish the upper edge by hand, turning the edges under and blindstitching the lining in place, Chapter 1, plate 15.

5 & 6. The tiny velvet bag and the lamé are both miniatures of bags with handles in Chapter 5. The tortoiseshell handles are a smaller version of the wooden rod and finial. The rings are two silver bangle bracelets that were lying unused in the bottom of a jewelry box, plate 15.

Both bags are cut in two pieces and mitered at the lower corners about 1½ inches across. We cut the velvet bag 8 inches wide x 10 inches long, allowing it to gather slightly on the rod. The handles are made of 1-inch-wide velvet ribbon backed with grosgrain. The decoration is described in Chapter 14. The ring bag is 10 inches wide at the top, slanted to 12 inches wide at the bottom to give a little extra room.

Both bags are interfaced with lightweight Pellon® and lined with silk, finished by hand. The basic construction was done by machine, using the ideas in Chapter 5.

14

From Grandma's Scrap Bag

Way back when pretty things were harder to come by and it wasn't easy to run down to the store to buy them, Grandma was wonderfully inventive. She kept the bright bits of calico and gingham and the scraps of Grandpa's shirting and she put them all together to make quilts or pillows or aprons. Patchwork and piecework and appliqué became art forms —created of necessity.

Now a lot of people can afford to throw away the scraps, but they're learning that Grandma had the right idea, and so once again the scrap bag is becoming a source of inspiration to the artist. We've borrowed from the traditional American quilt designs and from the fabrics and designs of other countries to show what can be done to make bags beautiful with scraps, plate 6.

1. Fabric shops sometimes have cards of samples that they no longer need. We came by one of these that had two dozen Scottish wool tartans in nice 3-inch-x-6-inch pieces. If we had seamed them together, they would have become too small to be useful, so we decided to put them together with 1-inch-wide grosgrain ribbon in a muted tan that blended well with all the colors. We bought 7 yards and used almost all of it.

We cut a piece of medium-weight Pellon®, 14 inches x 38 inches, and began arranging and rearranging the pieces until the colors were pleasing. We pinned them in place, but you might find it useful to iron them down with strips of fusible web. The raw edges are almost ½ inch apart so that the ribbon covers at least ¼ inch of each edge. Stitch the short pieces of ribbon across first, 5 of them, covering all but the top and bottom of the 6 rows of patches. Then stitch the 3 long pieces to cover the sides of the patches.

Cut a lining to match the size of the flat bag, lay it wrong side together with the Pellon® backing, and bind the ends with folded ribbon. Fold the bag together across the center and bind the sides, letting the ribbon run across the top as long as you want for a handle. Made in this size our tartan bag is perfect for carrying magazines, papers, and manuscripts. See page 114.

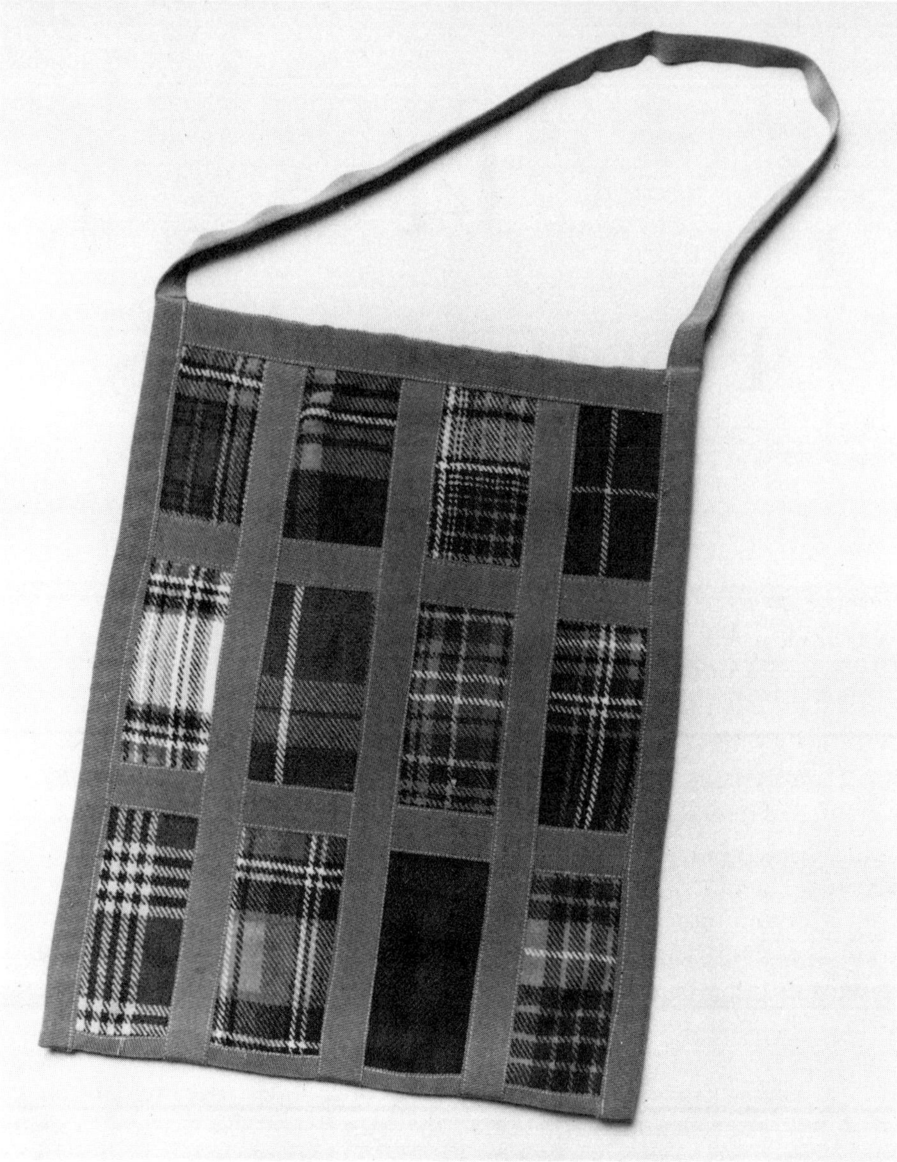

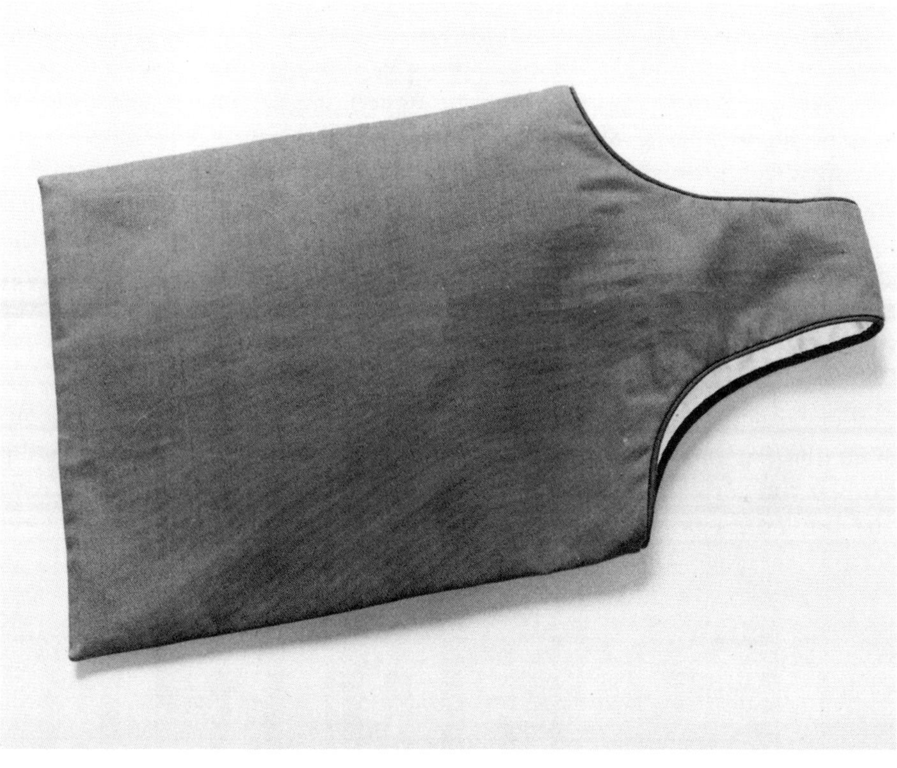

From Grandma's Scrap Bag 115

2. The flat bag with built-in handle offers a good surface for embroidery and decoration. The actual finished bag is almost square, 13 inches across by 13½ inches long, excluding the handle which rises 7 inches. Use the pattern shape for the top and handle and continue the side line down 13½ inches from the upper corner. Add seams all around before cutting. Cut two pieces of bag fabric and two pieces of lining fabric alike, plus interfacing if desired. Work all decoration or embroidery before assembling the bag.

a. Seam the back and front of the bag and the back and front of the lining together identically along all the straight edges. There are two little tricks that make finishing the curved edges by hand easy. Stitch a fine corded piping (Chapter 9, page 90) around the curves on the outer bag. Staystitch the lining along the seamline on the curve. Clip both edges and press them under along the stitched lines. Blindstitch the lining in place, wrong side together with the bag.

Half-size pattern.
Scale up and add seams.

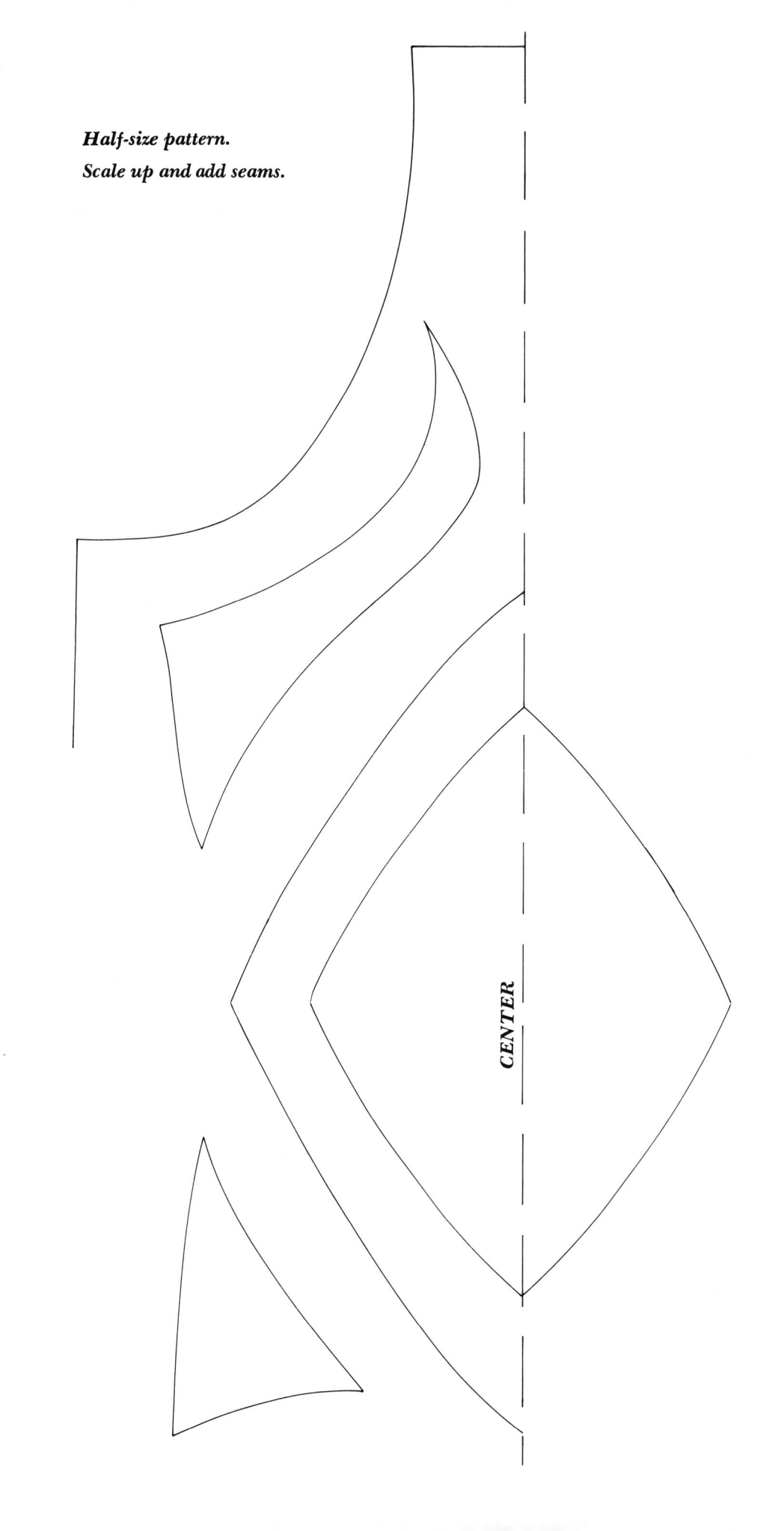

CENTER

b. Our reverse appliqué diagram should be used as a suggestion for your own monogram or design. We used a firm dark-brown poplin for the bottom layer, then proceeded with red, yellow, blue, and topped it off with green, all in lightweight cotton. These can be pinned or basted together around the edge, plate 5.

If you use our design as a basis for your own, trace the outline of each shape lightly on the top fabric, then baste ½ inch outside the line. Cut the fabric away ¼ inch inside each marking, clip carefully back to each corner, and turn the edges under. Finger press along the folds and baste if it makes it feel more secure. Blindstitch around, taking a few extra stitches in the corners, if necessary.

We wanted a graded width effect to our colors, so we cut the next layer ⅝ inch and turned the raw edge back to meet the first stitching; the next layer ½ inch; and the next layer ⅜ inch. In the corner shapes we started at the ½-inch level and went down to ⅜ inch, omitting the yellow altogether. As you work with the reverse appliqué, you will decide when to cut a layer away completely and then, of course, you can build back up in the center with whichever colors you wish. The monogram is relatively easy to work out. Draw your own inside the inner shape given on the pattern. We built the side letters back up in red and yellow and the center one in blue and green. We allowed only ⅛ inch turn-under on each layer of the letters—so the work is more delicate than with the outer shapes. If this seems beyond your patience, try a simpler decoration in the center.

3. The boat and tote bag is described on page 42. The pieced schooner is made and sewed on before the seams are sewed. Add ¼ inch

Full-size patterns.
Add seams.

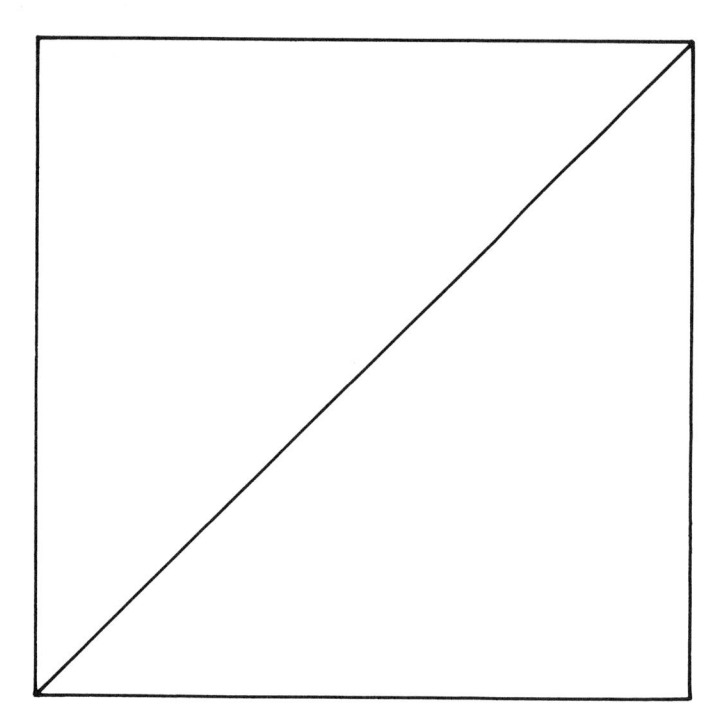

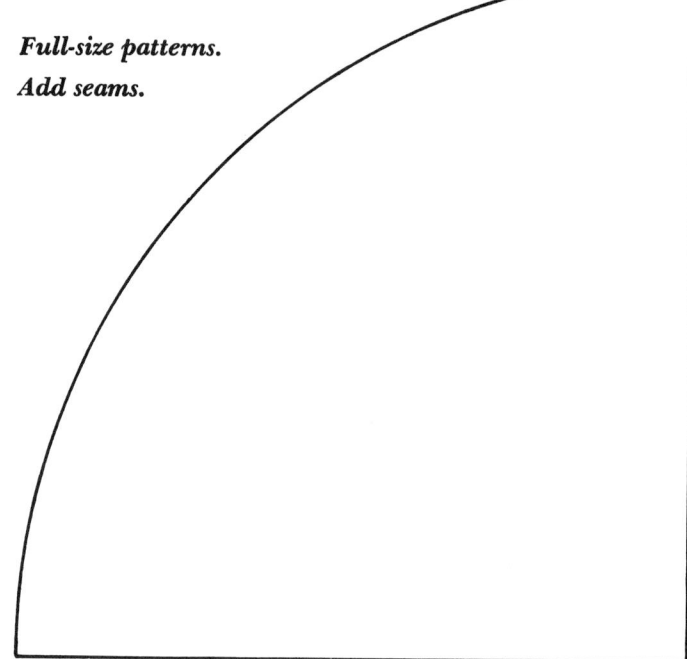

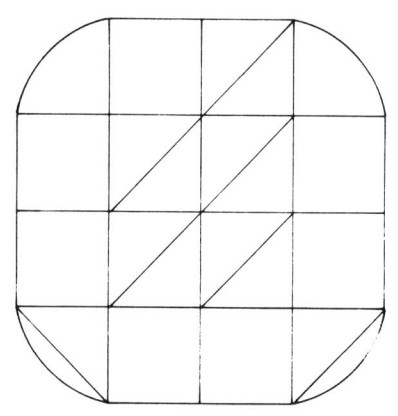

Scaled piecing diagram.

to all the pieces when cutting. The best way to do this is the way Grandma did it. Make cardboard patterns from the square, triangle, and corner piece. Draw around these on the wrong side of the fabric and cut ¼ inch outside of the lines. Cut 7 squares and 7 triangles in calico print, round the corners of 2 of each by the corner pattern. Cut 2 red squares and 2 red triangles and 5 yellow squares. Seam the pieces together on the machine according to the piecing diagram. Stitch medium-size rickrack on the right side of the fabric on the outside seamline. Turn the seam under so that half the rickrack extends around the edge. Pin the design in place on the front of the bag rectangle and stitch it in place through the rickrack close to the turned edge.

4. The book bag is made by the directions for the swim and gym bag on page 62, omitting the back pocket. The schoolhouse design is an old

Full-size patterns.
Add seams.

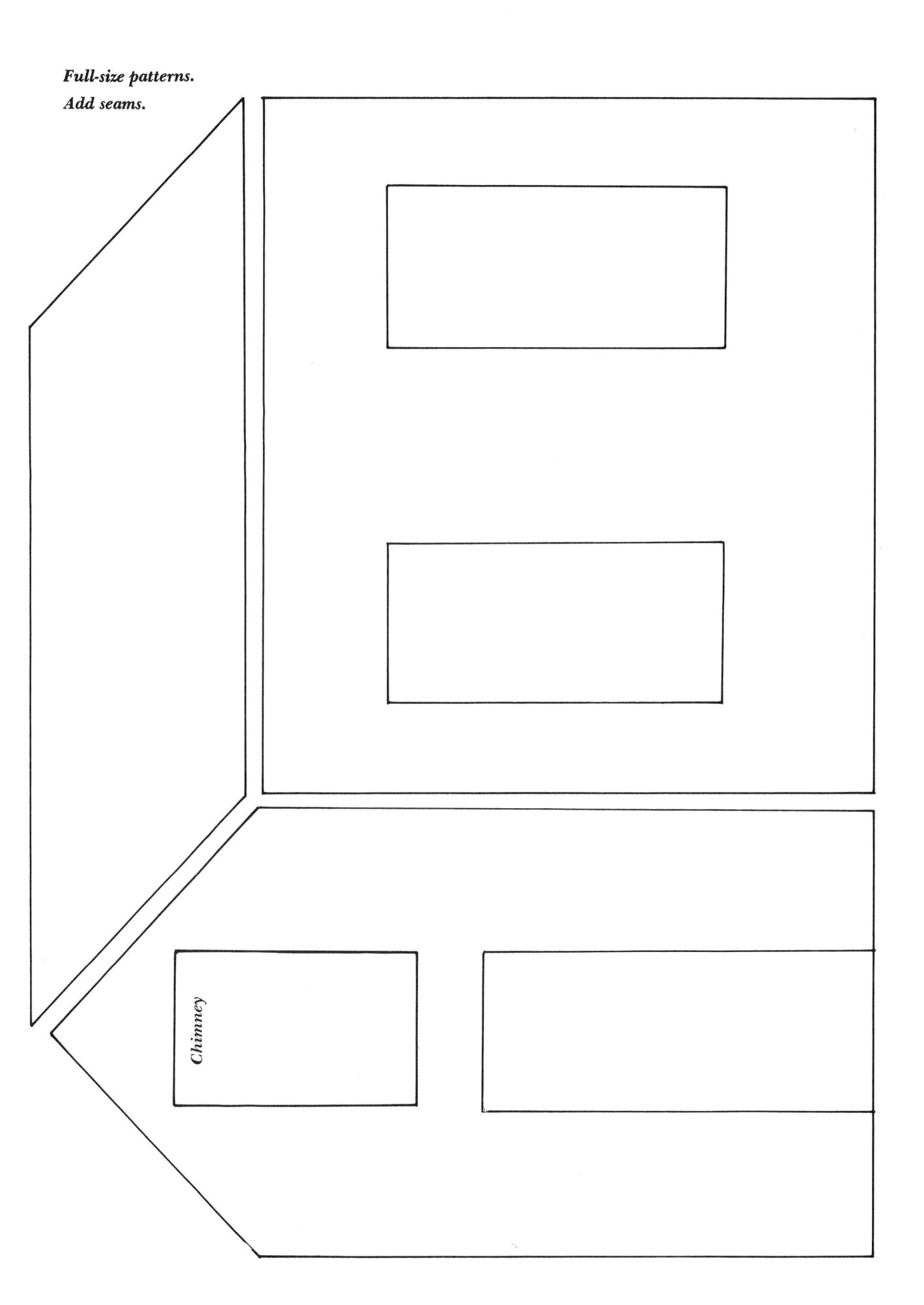

Chimney

and very traditional quilt pattern. We used three calico prints and applied the pieces with a machine zigzag stitch.

Cut the windows and door of one print, allowing ¼-inch seam all around. Cut the main building pieces of another print, allowing ¼-inch seam all around. Lay the window and door pieces under the openings on the main pieces and pin all pieces in place. Using a wide zigzag stitch, work over the seamlines all around the main pieces. Trim away the excess with fine, sharp scissors. Cut the roof and chimney pieces from another print, allowing seam all around, and zigzag them in place. Trim the edges.

5. The same backpack that we made in heavy canvas on page 69 can become city-wise with some happy quilted appliqué. The fabric is a firm chino made for rainwear. The "Moon Over the Mountain" design is usually seen as a quilt square, but we felt it looked better rounded in the square frame of the pack flap. Because the fabric is light in weight, we welted the seams (Chapter 1) for added strength.

Cut the three shapes in appropriate colors—blue sky, yellow moon, and green mountain—adding ¼-inch seams all around. Cut all three pieces again in Pellon® Fleece, omitting seams. Turn under the outer edge of the sky and blindstitch it in place. Slip the Pellon® under it and quilt out in rays like moonbeams. Repeat the process with the moon piece, covering the raw edge of the sky, and quilt around in circles. Repeat again with the mountain piece, covering the last raw edges and turning the curved edge over the Pellon®. Quilt in lines down from the point.

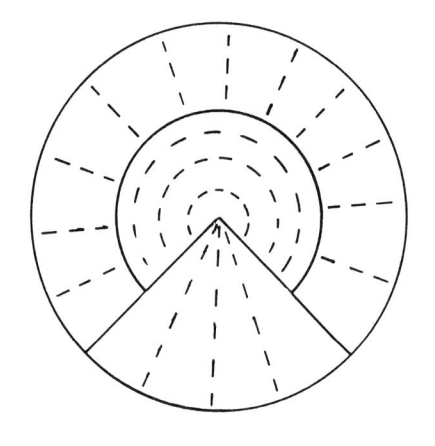

Scaled piecing diagram.

Full-size patterns.

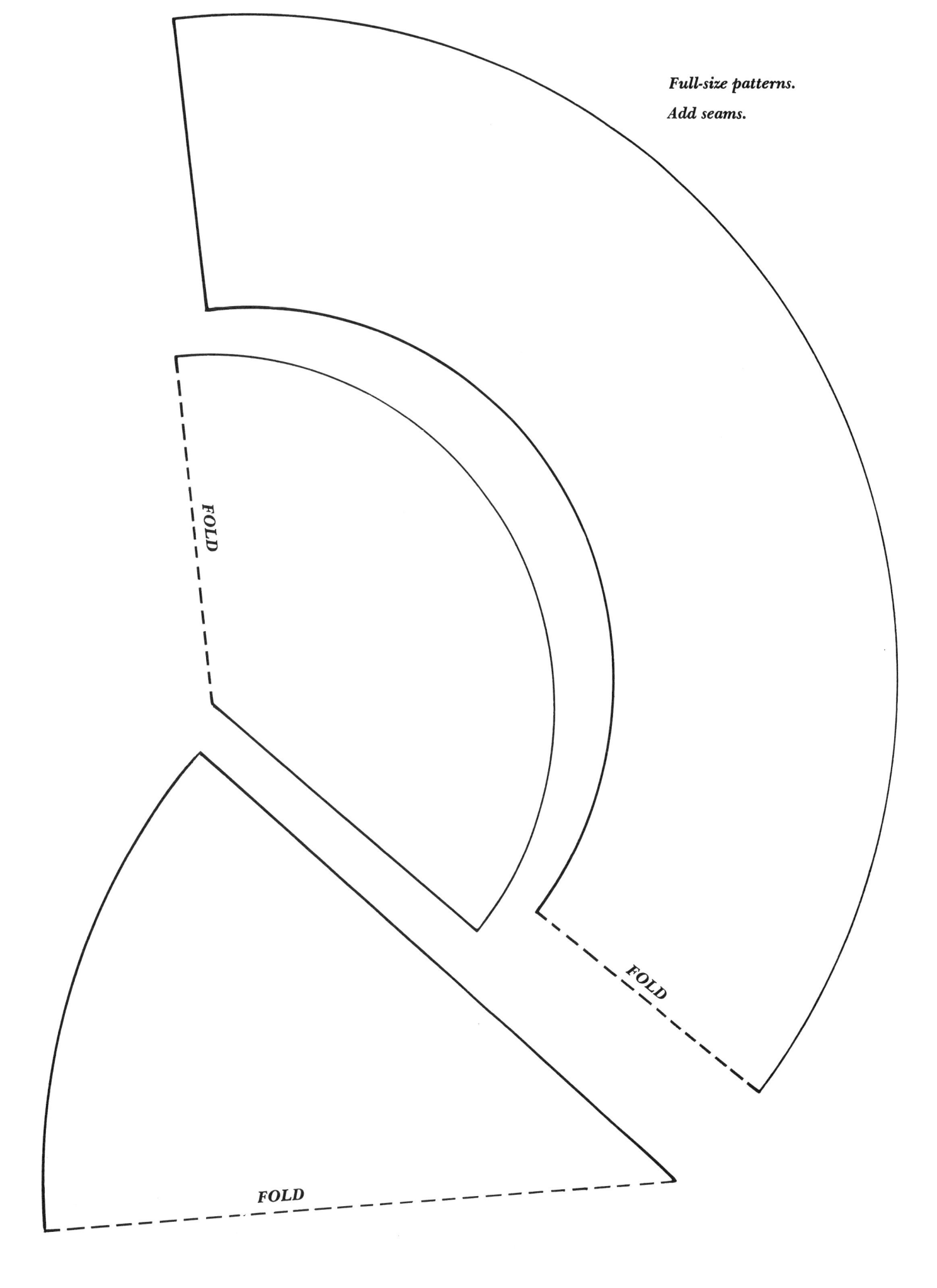

Add seams.

FOLD

FOLD

FOLD

15

Yours Personally

Monograms not only personalize bags but decorate them easily and delightfully. We felt that what was needed was an alphabet that was easy to translate into many kinds of embroidery. That meant it had to have simple lines, preferably curved, and that it had to be easy to blow up to a larger size without losing anything. The one we have here—in 2-inch-high size—works beautifully as is, delicately beaded, or in a gigantic 6-inches, padded to look even larger.

Needleworkers often seem timid about scaling up designs to larger sizes, so we have given you a handy on-the-spot aid, two larger-size grids over which to work. It's easy to increase the 2-inch alphabet to 4 inches on the ½-inch grid or to 6 inches on the ¾-inch grid. Trace or Xerox the letters you want to use and the section of ¼-inch grid that is under them. With these beside you as a guide, lay a piece of tissue paper over the larger-size grid and copy each curve of the letter as it appears in its square. The first try may be a little rough and jumpy-looking, but you can tidy it up with a curved ruler or French curve. It's not a big job. After all, you need only two or three letters at a time. We threw in the numbers so that you can date your handiwork or include a memorable date for a friend.

Whether you prefer to work by hand or on your sewing machine, you can embroider the smoothly shaped initials on many fabrics. If a fabric is soft or limp, you may find it easier to back it with Pellon® or with a woven interfacing fabric before starting.

The first step is always to draw the monogram onto tissue paper. You can then trace it onto the fabric with a knitting needle and dressmaker's carbon or by stitching through the tissue onto the fabric, outlining the letters.

We worked monograms or individual letters in six techniques. Here are instructions and tips for the ones we created.

1. Appliqué is easier to work with the larger letters than with the 2-inch ones. If you plan to work by machine, as we did, you will trace the letters onto the right side of the appliqué fabric. Don't cut them out on the outline but at least ½ inch outside it. Pin the letters in place on

A B C D

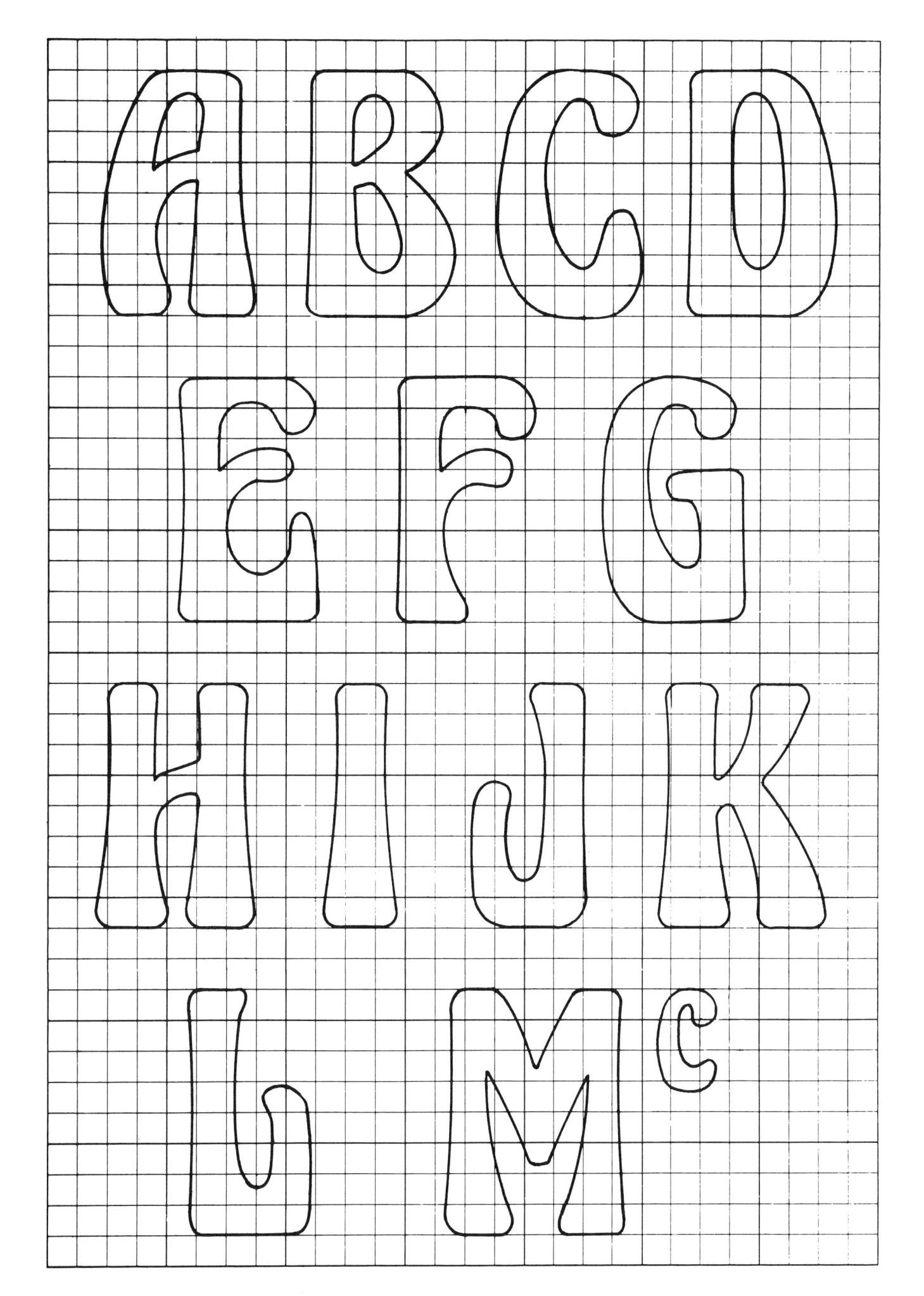

E F G

H I J K

L M

N O P
Q R S T
U V W
X Y Z

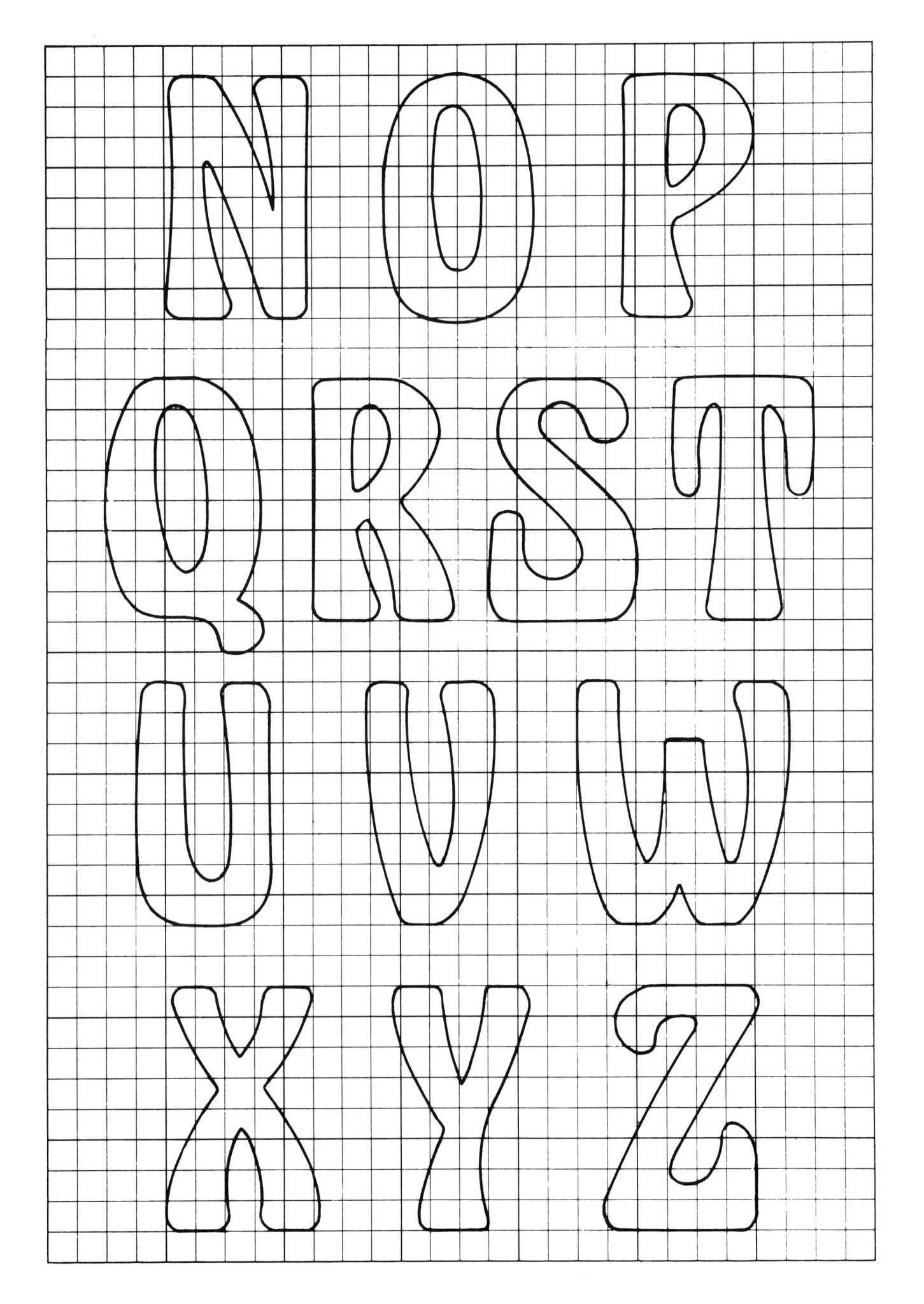

1 2 3
4 5 6
7 8 9
0 &

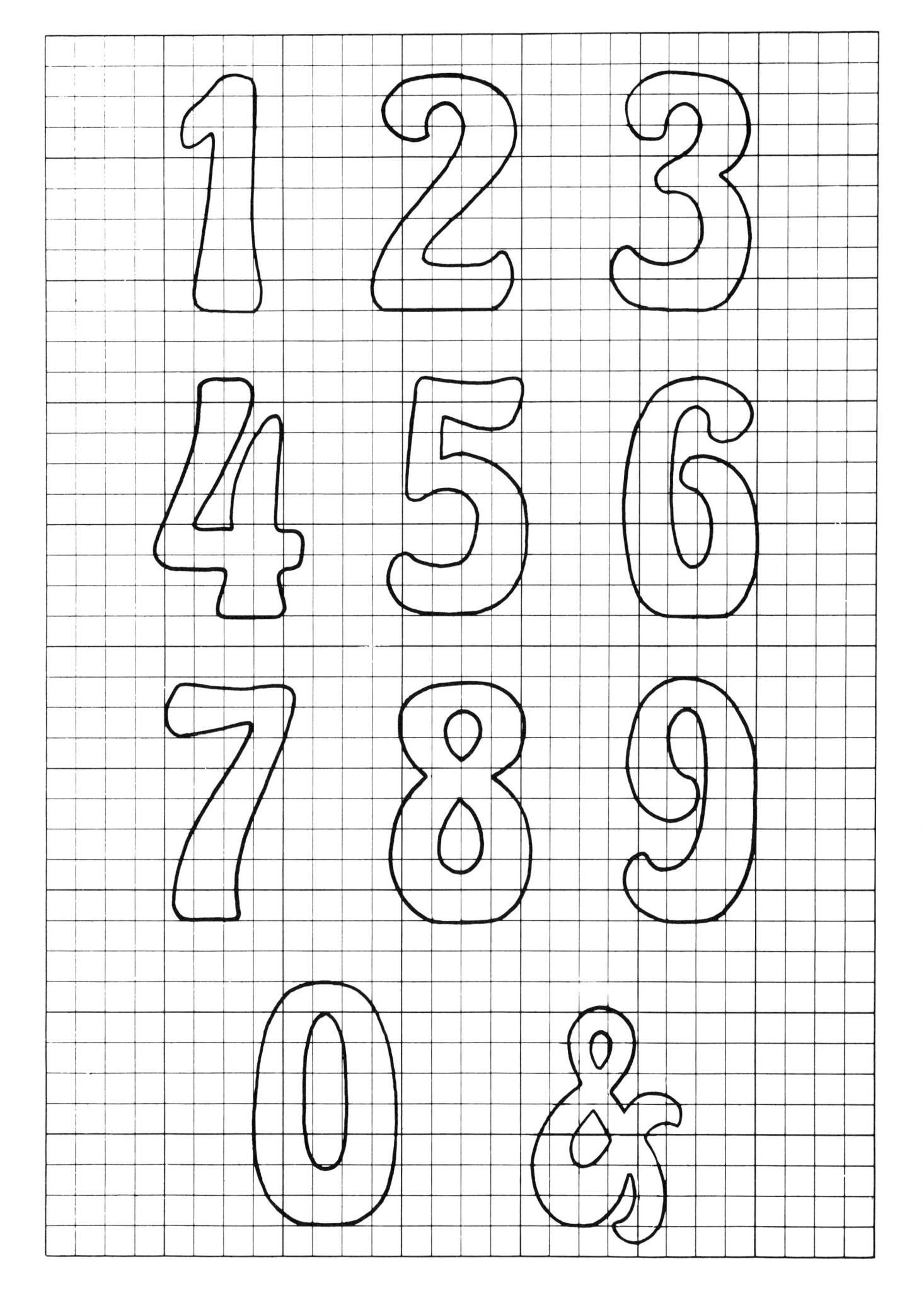

½-inch grid

¾-inch grid

the bag fabric. Set the zigzag on the machine for a wide width and about 15 stitches to the inch. Stitch around each letter over the traced line. Trim away all excess fabric as close as possible to the stitching.

If you wish to appliqué by hand, trace the letters onto the wrong side of the appliqué fabric. Using the straight stitch on the sewing machine, stitch just outside the line. Trim away the fabric $1/4$ inch outside the line. The stitching makes it easier to turn the edge under and baste it. You will then pin it to the bag fabric and blindstitch the turned edge in place by hand.

2. Padded quilting is now sometimes called "soft sculpture" and creates a very modern and interesting large monogram. Lay a piece of thin woven interfacing fabric on the wrong side of the bag fabric in the

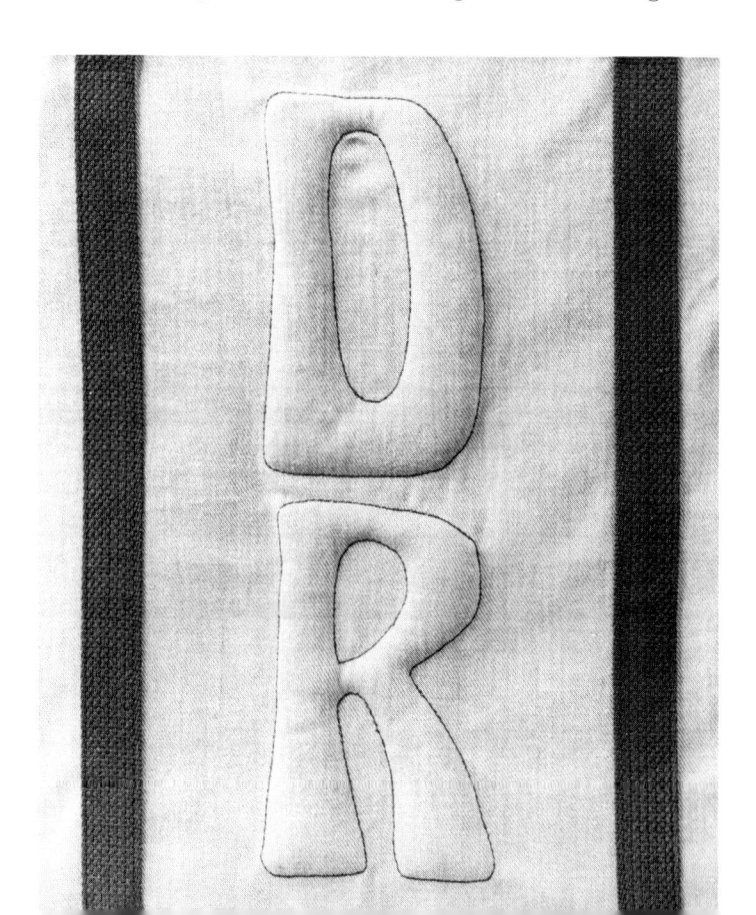

area to be embroidered. Pin it in place. Lay tissue paper—onto which you have drawn the letters—on the right side of the bag fabric in the same area. Machine stitch along the lines through all three layers. We used buttonhole twist in a darker shade (on the top of the machine only, with regular sewing thread in the bobbin). When the stitching meets at the point where it started, pull all the threads through to the wrong side and tie them off securely.

Tear the tissue off. Cut a very small slit in the lining fabric at about the center of each letter. Use a crochet hook or knitting needle to push small pieces of polyester filling into the cavity of the letter. Work it up into the corners and get it smooth and even but not overstuffed. If you plan to use stiffening in the bag, it will go on at this point. There is no need to close the slits; the filling has no tendency to leak out.

3. Soutache braid makes a delicate outlined initial. Trace the letters onto the right side of the bag fabric, using light dressmaker's carbon on dark fabrics and dark on light. Hold the braid over the line and stitch it in place. We did it on the machine, but it can just as well be done by hand with a backstitch. The beginning and end of the braid should be overlapped about ½ inch and tacked together.

4. Machine embroidery can be done in different ways on different machines, including some straight-stitch machines. We can cover only a small part of this information here, so we suggest that you read your sewing-machine manual. Our monogram was worked on a relatively simple zigzag machine, so we will give you these basic tips.

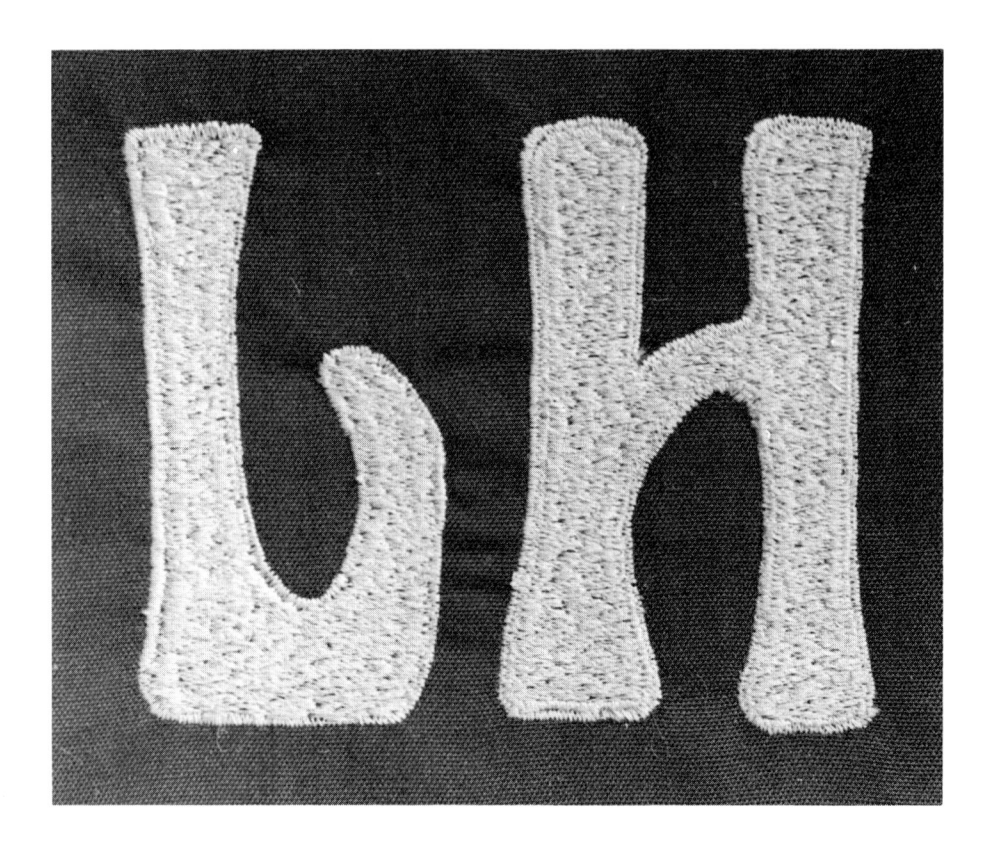

Be sure your machine is clean and oiled. Run test pieces of the fabric and thread that you're planning to use. Cotton and cotton-blend fabrics in medium to heavy weight work best. If your fabric puckers, it is probably too lightweight—back it with an interfacing fabric. We find that cotton thread made especially for machine embroidery is almost foolproof, and the newer polyesters work much better than the first ones on the market.

Trace your letters onto the bag fabric by straight stitching through the lines drawn on tissue paper. Tear the paper away. Set the zigzag for a medium width and a fine length. Lay the fabric right side up on the large part of an embroidery hoop and slip the small part in, so that the fabric will be flat on the machine. You may need to remove the presser foot to slide the hoop under the needle, then screw the foot back in place on the bar. Work a zigzag line all the way around over the straight stitching.

For the inside filler stitching you will work free-hand. This technique varies greatly with different machines and always requires practice to get the rhythm of the hand motion. In most cases it is necessary to cover or drop the feed teeth, remove the presser foot, and lower the presser bar—just as though the foot were still on. On most zigzag machines you will set the stitch to the widest width and a neutral length and work the fabric with a side-to-side swinging motion. On straight-stitch machines it is often possible to do the same kind of stitching but without the zigzag

Yours Personally 131

border around. The motion is usually a back-and-forth one, but please read your machine manual.

5. If you're more comfortable with handwork in front of the TV, you can work a very similar type of monogram with rows of chain stitch. Ours is done in Persian wool on a wool bag, but pearl thread or six-strand will work quite well on cotton or linen. Trace the letters onto the bag fabric with dressmaker carbon or by machine stitching and tearing away the paper. Work the first line of chain stitch over the traced line. Continue to work lines close inside the first one until the entire surface is filled. We suggest that you use a book of simple embroidery stitches to find other kinds of filler for large monograms. Couched gold threads are lovely for evening, or use a dainty lattice filler on a summer linen.

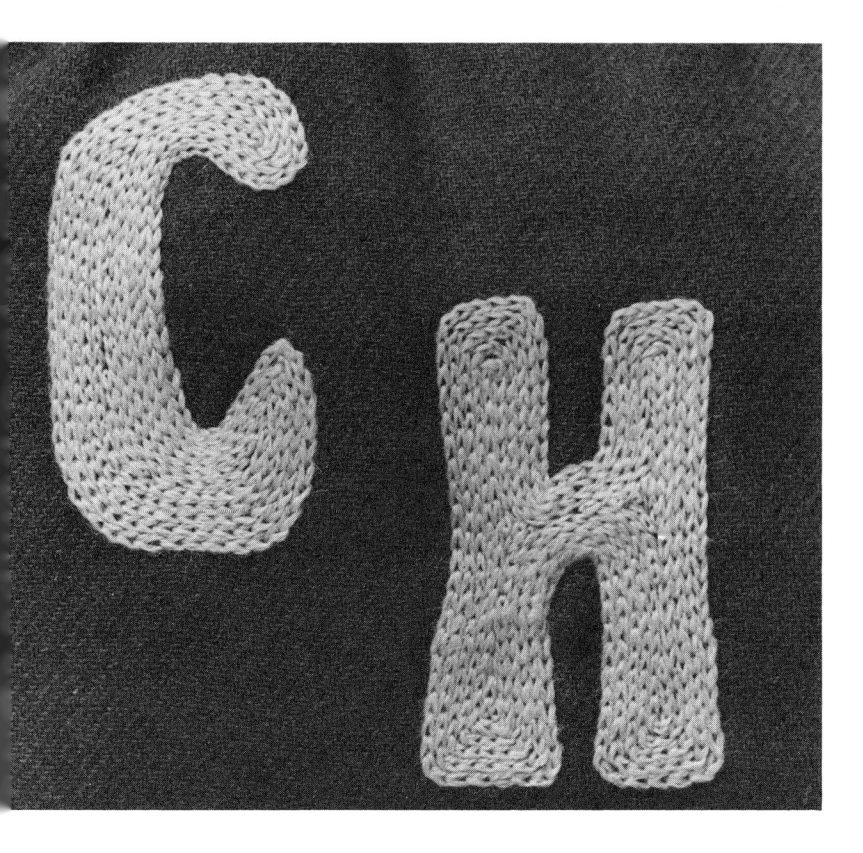

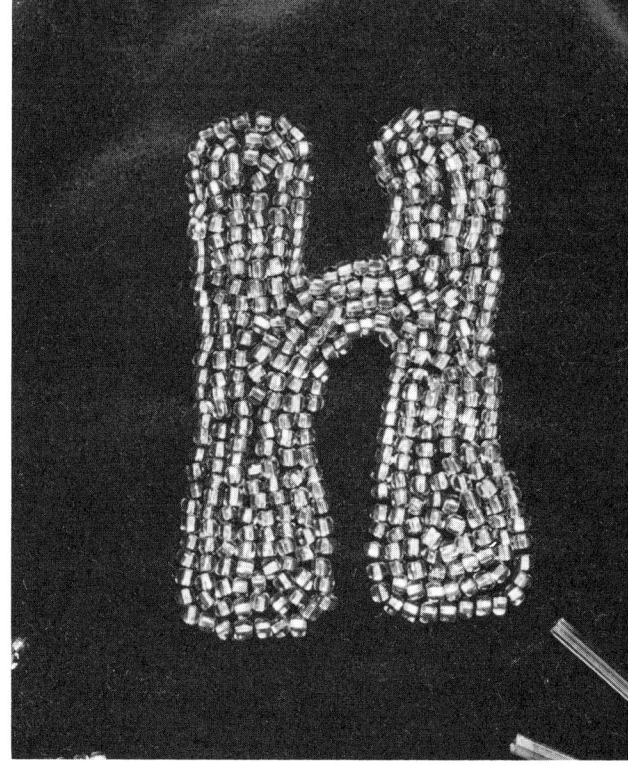

6. The beaded initial is almost like the chain-stitch one, simply a matter of working rows around and around, starting with the outside. We found it best to make the letter in reverse on a piece of batiste backing which we basted onto the wrong side of the velvet. The surface of velvet wriggles too much to get a clear marking of any kind on it. This means that only on the first row you must keep referring to the back of the work to see where to insert the needle. After that you're off and running.

Be sure to use a beading needle—very long and thin—and fine strong thread, such as polyester. Do not use the "invisible" extruded nylon thread. The small round glass beads available in variety stores are just right for working around curves. The longer straight ones are showy and nice for the starbursts, because they work up quickly.

Use a backstitch to sew the beads in place. It takes a few minutes of practice to get the stitches close enough and even. Each time you bring the needle up to the right side of the fabric you will thread a bead on and insert the needle the width of the bead back of the point where you brought it up. Bring the needle up the width of a bead beyond this bead, thread on a bead, and insert the needle back at the last bead. Once you have the outline covered, you will fill the center with close rows, as with the chain stitch. The closer you pack the beading together, the smoother the final effect will be.

Because we feel that artistic freedom is important to the personal statement of anything that you make, we only suggest the starbursts as a background for your initial. They are made by grouping several larger round beads for the center and then making as many spokes of either small beads or long ones as you wish. You could just as well work scroll designs or make a two- or three-letter monogram. Beading seems rather slow at first, but there is so much glitter and effect for so little work that you should find it a perfect way of turning a scrap of glamorous fabric into a luxury gift.

16

Cheap, Quick Fun

Dress up a gift with a gift bag made just for the occasion. They're quick and inexpensive, often costing no more than gift wrapping, and they have that personal touch that everyone finds flattering.

The trick is to use easy shapes, available materials, and omit all fancy linings and trimmings. Burlap, muslin, and leftover scraps are logical choices. An inexpensive felt, made of washable polyester and called Phun Phelt®, is extra easy to work with because it requires no finishing.

The purpose of these bags is not to be lasting or even very useful. They should be happy, fitted to the item they contain, and inventive. Use the directions for any tote bag, flat bag, or drawstring bag in this book and translate it into quick-and-easy. Measure the slippers, the large toy, whatever the gift, and make the bag to contain it.

Here are a few tips for the ones we have made:

1. The tote bags are both made in Phun Phelt®. The boat design is applied with fusible web. The Christmas tree is held in place by the stitching which runs through the gold braid. The upper edges of both are hemmed for added strength. The handles are backed with grosgrain ribbon to give the bags a little longer life than that of paper wrappings, plate 11.

2. The man's slipper bag is made just like the shoe bags in Chapter 11 but in burlap. Iron-on mending tape comes in lots of colors and makes great instant appliqué. We used the monograms from Chapter 15 and the little footprint designs given in this chapter and ironed them on before stitching the bag together, plate 9.

3. The tiny gold money bag is made in the same way from a scrap of synthetic leather and makes a special gift of a small amount of money for a child. Someone suggested it might be a nice way to give a handful of diamonds, too, plate 8.

4. The wine bottle cover is made by drawing around the bottle to get the shape of the bottom circle (Chapter 2) and then cutting the side

Full-size patterns.

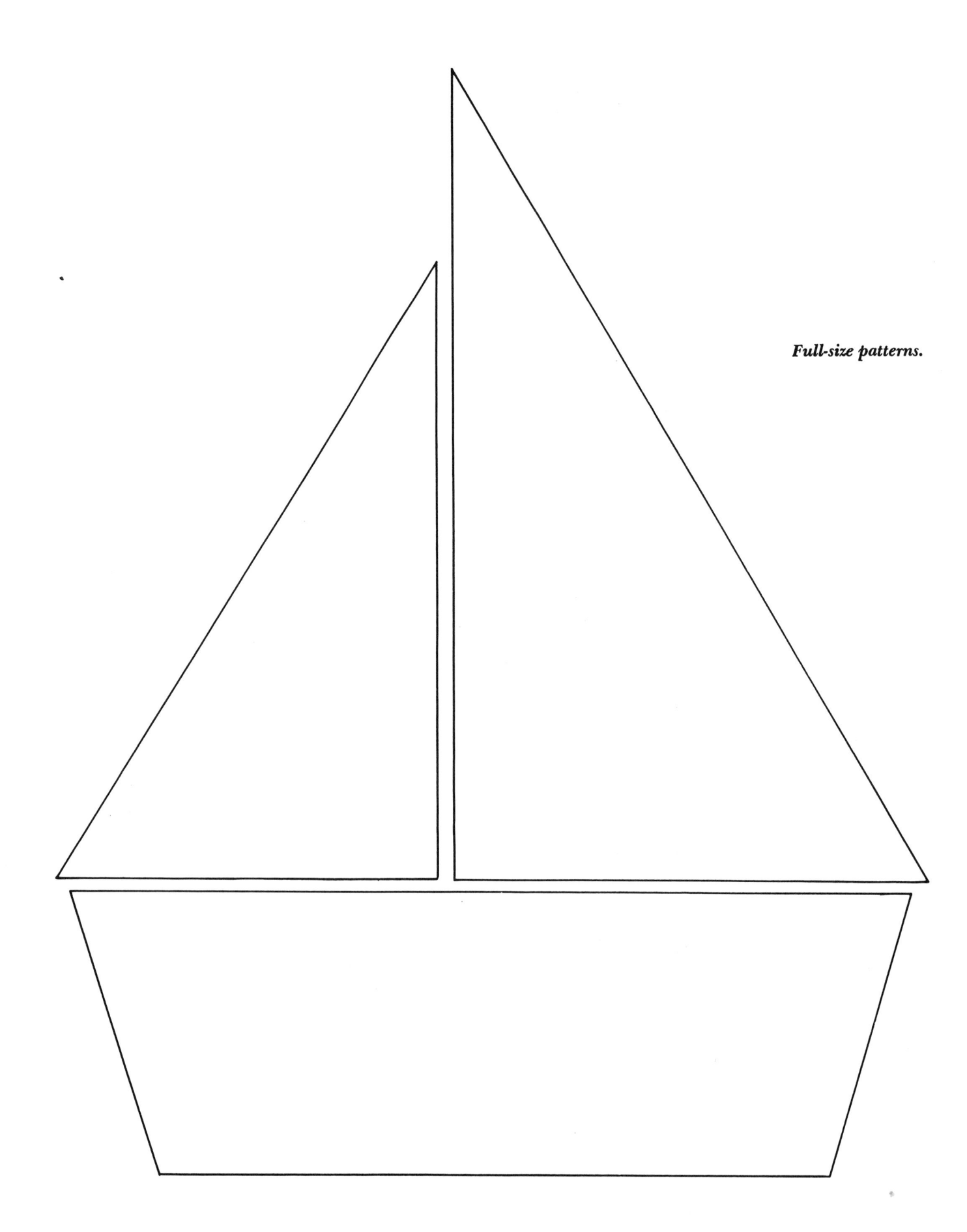

Cheap, Quick Fun 135

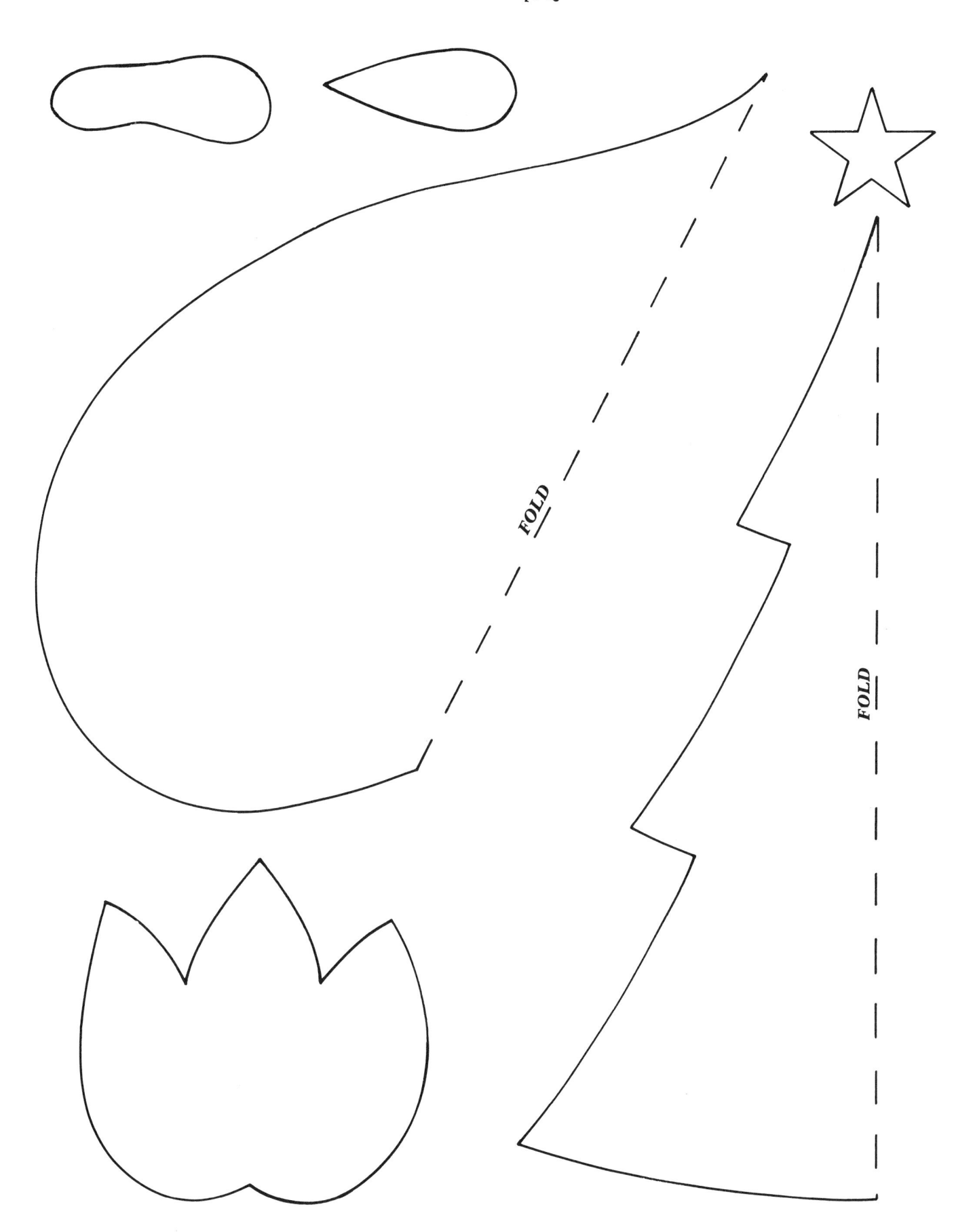

FOLD

FOLD

piece a fraction larger than the circumference of the bottle and easing it to the circular bottom. The grape-leaf design is given here and the grapes are circles the size of a dime, all cut of iron-on mending tape, plate 9.

5. The hearts-and-flowers bag is perfect for a valentine gift or at any time for perfume or jewelry. The daisy is fused on and the handles are made of scraps of velvet ribbon, plate 8.

6. To make a wrap-up book cover, cut the Phun Phelt® by the shape of the dust jacket, allowing about ¼ inch extra at the top and bottom of the book so that the flaps can be stitched to the outside. Make wraparound handles of any ribbon or peasant braid. Make a snap fastening of the same ribbon so that the book will be closed tightly, plate 8.

7. A heavy grade of muslin makes a money envelope that will last and do double duty as a checkbook cover. Measure a pocket checkbook—ours was 3 inches x 6½ inches. We cut the fabric 12½ inches x 7½ inches. Turn the short ends under ¼ inch and stitch. Fold them back right sides together 3 inches from each stitched end and seam them. When you turn the ends right side out again, there will be a 3-inch-deep pocket at each end. We stenciled the initials on with fabric paint before stitching, plate 8.

A word about fabric coloring: There are several brands of fabric paint on the market. All come with very complete instructions. The plastic sheets of letters and shapes available in stationery stores are easy to use with a stencil brush. Practice a little and use lots of paper towels to keep from having regrets.

Ordinary wax crayons can be used effectively to color fabrics such as muslin. Use the color heavily, then iron the fabric between several layers of paper towels until the wax has melted out. There are also crayons made specifically to be used in this way, not always as easy to come by as the ones in the children's toy chests.

If you enjoy coloring in this way, there is no reason why you can't color any of the larger designs, such as the two turnabout bags. Buy stencil paper at an art store and cut the designs from it and use a stencil brush or crayons just as you would in commercially cut stencils.

8. Turnabout bags are just-for-fun gifts or conversation pieces for yourself. The rain-or-shine one has the designs appliquéd on by machine. Use a medium-width, fine-length zigzag stitch as described for the game-board bag, page 66. We used a heavy grade of muslin and covered it after appliquéing with medium-weight pliable plastic. The bag is cut 12 inches x 28 inches (folding to 12 inches x 14 inches) and trimmed with wide bias binding (Chapter 1), plate 10.

The political bag is for people who can't make up their minds. We made it of Phun Phelt®, backed with fusible Pellon® so that it will last at least through one political campaign. The designs are stitched on with a machine straight stitch and the bag is trimmed with fold-braid (Chapter 1), plate 10.

The designs can be used on other bags of any size and enlarged or made smaller. If you have a friend who is a dedicated party worker, perhaps you might make a more lasting bag with the correct political symbol.

Full-size patterns.

Add seams.

Cheap, Quick Fun 139

Full-size patterns.

Cheap, Quick Fun   141

17

Everything Is Fair Game

There's no rule that says you have to go out and buy an exact amount of just the right fabric for a bag. Anything that you see and like and that suggests a bag to your mind may be just what you want. Our list includes mosquito net, an assortment of straw mats and baskets, parts of our most beloved worn-out jeans, and a "Hoboken oriental" rug. Some of them are made by the directions for totes and other basic bags. In other cases it was necessary for us to let the shape of the item itself dictate its shape and style.

1 & 2. String bags and other fold-up bags that can be tucked in your purse are awfully useful when you go out shopping. We found that inexpensive nylon mosquito net—sold in camping-goods stores—made ones that fold into a tiny corner and pop out to carry the week's groceries or the yarn and directions for a new sweater.

The larger tote bag is made by the directions for the big blue tote on page 42. We cut the straps 28 inches, which is long enough to go over the shoulder, in case you're running short of hands. We double-stitched the side seams, incorporating a piece of ¼-inch-wide twill tape for extra strength.

The other bag is cut like the flat bag with handles (page 26). The ends are bound with fold-braid and the edges are bound with a continuous piece of fold-braid which also forms the handles (Chapter 1). We stitched the handle edges wrong sides together, incorporating a piece of ¼-inch twill tape. We used 2½ yards of fold-braid in all.

3. The carpet bag was made entirely by hand because we couldn't get it under the machine needle without a battle. It has side panels and a rod and finial finish, somewhat like the brown canvas bag, page 56. The rug is only 22 inches x 36 inches and very inexpensive. We bought two ⅜-inch diameter dowels to replace the shorter ones that came with the nice big wooden finials. The dowels had to be cut to 23 inches to fit the width of the bag. We also used 2 yards of 2-inch-wide tan webbing for the side panels and strap handles.

We cut the side panels 15 inches long and hemmed them 1 inch

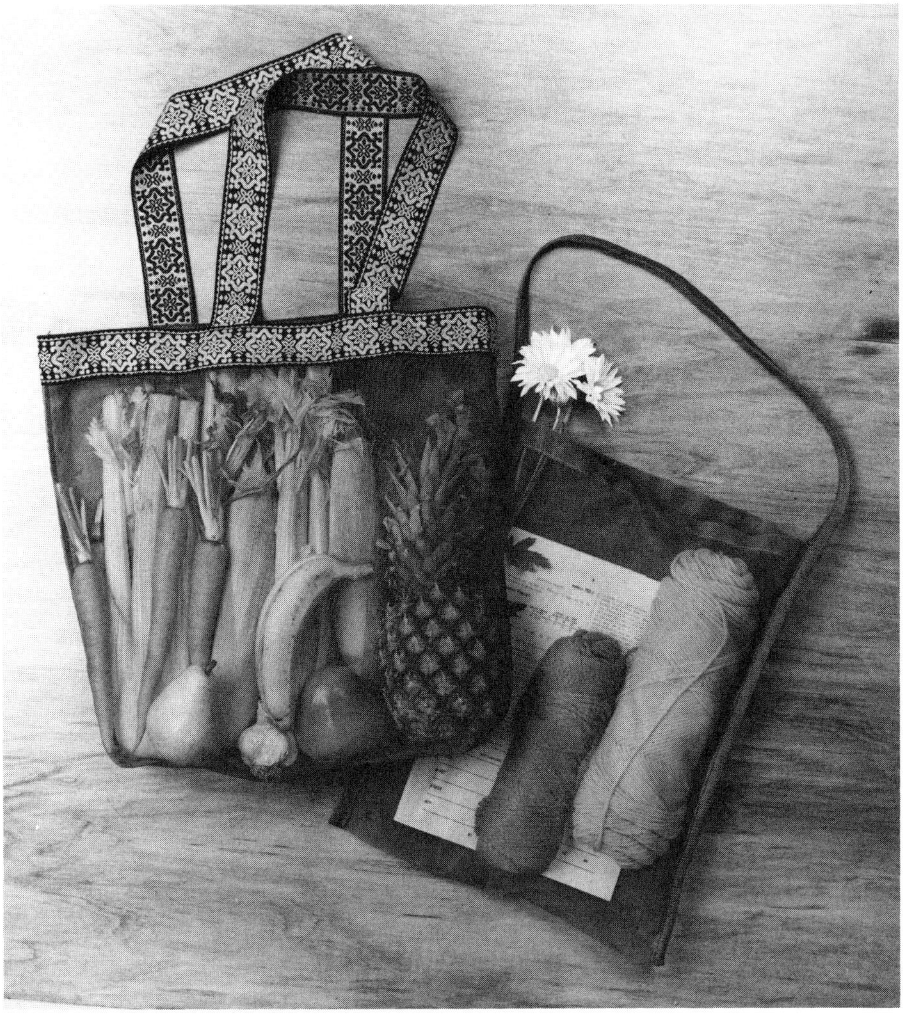

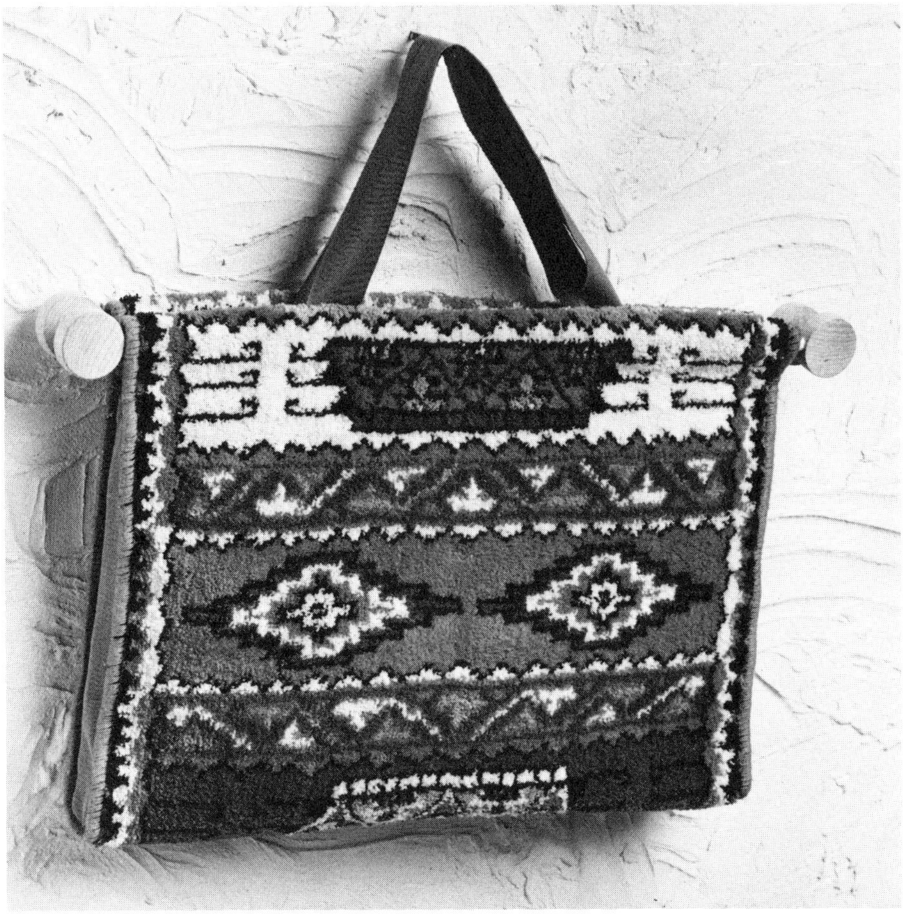

deep at top and bottom for added strength. Mark and match them as you would for any side-panel tote (page 36). We found that a strong needle and carpet thread made sewing a little easier, but it is one of those projects that will send you running for a thimble if you've never used one before. It was worth the effort, though, because it makes a terrific and unusual art portfolio, large enough, strong enough, and startling enough in appearance.

4. Odds and ends of old jeans, especially the leg sections of cutoffs, cry to be used for something—a bag, of course. By piecing together dark blue, light blue, and wheat color we were able to make this flat bag with wraparound handles. The center panel is 8 inches wide; the whole bag is 11 inches deep, 14 inches across at the bottom, and 18 inches across at the top. The slanted shape was suggested by a flat, woven Indian bag that we saw in a museum. The pockets had to be cut from a pair of jeans totally worn-out—they were not removed by ripping the stitching.

We seamed all the pieces together, then cut fusible Pellon® and checked gingham lining to fit. It took 3½ yards of peasant braid ⅝ inch wide to trim the upper edge and make the handles, which are double in the part that comes above the bag. After the outer fabric was fused to the

Everything Is Fair Game 145

Pellon® and the handles attached to within 2 inches of the top, we seamed the bag together, seamed the lining together, and dropped the lining into the bag. We finished the top with the braid and stitched the other layer onto the back of the handle extensions. We then finished stitching the handles to the bag all the way to the top.

5. The little basket bag with the tied-over handles is the sort of suggestion that you will have to adapt to your own basket. Our basket measured 20 inches around the inside of the rim. We cut 8 pieces of batik by the pattern (page 146), seamed them together in pairs, and turned them all right side out. Using heavy-duty thread, double in the needle, we attached them to the inside of the rim, working in and out of the weave of the straw. We then shaped a lining to fit the inside of the bag. You can do this by pinning a piece or two pieces of fabric wrong side out over the outside of the basket, using seams or darts to shape it. Stitch the seams or darts slightly deeper than you pinned them and it will fit the inside. Turn the upper edge under and stitch the lining over the raw ends of the ties.

Full-size pattern.
Add seams.

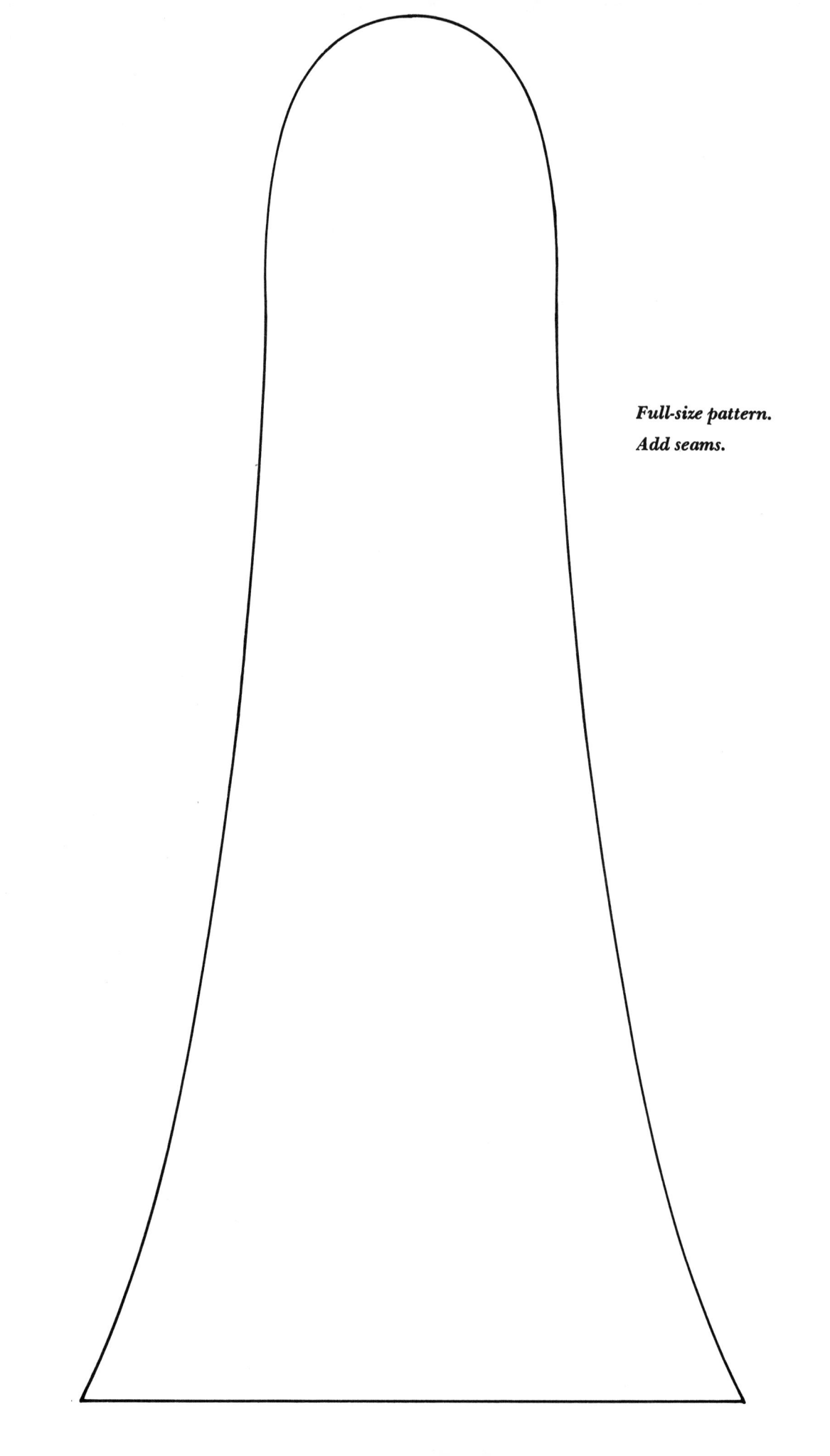

Everything Is Fair Game 147

6. The other basket bag is a self-lined one which can be made from a bowl-shaped basket of any size.

a. Measure the circumference of the basket. Cut a piece of medium-weight fabric that width plus seams, and twice as long as you want the fabric upper section to be when finished, plus the depth of the basket. If you're uncertain of the effect you want, cut longer, not shorter, than you think you want—it's easy to trim off. Seam the piece together to fit tightly around the upper edge of the basket. Using heavy-duty thread doubled in the needle, overcast the tube of fabric firmly to the upper edge of the basket as shown. Run two rows of gathering thread around the other end of the tube.

b. Cut a small, round piece of fabric, the size of the bottom of the basket plus seams. Turn the edges of the round piece under and baste them in place. Mark and match the pieces as described in the round gathered bag, page 30. Pull the gathering threads to fit the end of the tube to the circle. Pin the circle over the gathers and blindstitch it in place by hand.

148   **THE BIG BAG BOOK**

c. Push the entire lining down into the bag until the circle is in place in the bottom of the basket. Pin the folded upper edge evenly and stitch twice around for a heading and casing as deep as you want. Because it is difficult to gauge the measurements ahead of time, you will probably find it easier to open an inch of the side seam at the casing now than to plot it when you stitch the side seam (Chapter 1).

d. Use medium-weight cable cord to run through the casing. The finished bag in the small size that we made is nice for a summer purse. If you want to use a larger basket and put heavier things into the finished bag, we suggest that you work over the rim of the basket a second time with a decorative thread after the fabric is pulled up right side out. You could even make a sort of cross-stitch design by overcasting around one way and then crossing back.

7. Two round, woven straw mats and a yard of cotton drapery fabric make a great round boxed bag, below. It has to be finished with outside bound seams and we felt that it really didn't need a zipper. Here's how it went together, step by step.

a. Cut two circles of Pellon®, slightly smaller than the mats, and glue one to the wrong side of each mat. We used medium-weight Pellon® and Sobo glue. Cut two circles of the fabric, the same size as the mats. Using a long machine stitch and a sharp needle, stitch the fabric wrong sides together with the mats, about ¼ inch from the edge.

b. Cut fabric handles 3 inches x 14 inches, fold, and stitch them to a finished width of 1 inch (Chapter 1). Stitch them to the outside of the mats, as shown. They must be far enough from the edge not to interfere with binding the edge.

150 THE BIG BAG BOOK

c. Plan for the size opening you want and cut the boxing strip to fit around the rest of the circle and about 3 inches wide. Cut and piece bias, 2½ inches wide, from the remaining fabric. Baste the boxing strip, then bind over the edge (Chapter 1).

d. Baste the other side onto the other edge of the boxing strip. Remember that accuracy is a must before stitching, because although the straw will stand up to being stitched, it will be weakened by any ripping out of stitches.

Sources

Braids and trimmings by William E. Wright are available at fabric stores, department stores, and major chains, including Sears Roebuck & Co., Montgomery Ward & Co., and J. C. Penney Co., Inc.

Braids and trimmings by Loewenthal Trimmings Co. are available at fabric stores and department stores.

Pacific Silvercloth®, tarnish-preventing fabric, is available at department stores and through Sears Roebuck and J. C. Penney catalogues.

Pellon® products are available at fabric stores, department stores, and J. C. Penney Co., Inc.

Bag handles by David Traum Notions Co. are available in notions and variety stores and wherever fabrics are sold, including J. C. Penney Co., Inc., and Sears Roebuck & Co.

Heavy, eighteen-ounce canvas may be mail-ordered from Jensen-Lewis in New York City. For a swatch card of two dozen colors and a price list write, enclosing one dollar, to:
    Jensen-Lewis
    156 7th Ave.
    New York, N.Y. 10011